WITHDRAWN

TREES OF LIFE

TREES OF LIFE

SAVING TROPICAL FORESTS AND THEIR BIOLOGICAL WEALTH

**KENTON MILLER and
LAURA TANGLEY**

BEACON PRESS   BOSTON

World Resources Institute is deeply grateful to the Florence and John Schumann Foundation for support for WRI Guides to the Environment.

Beacon Press
25 Beacon Street
Boston, Massachusetts 02108

Beacon Press books
are published under the auspices of
the Unitarian Universalist Association of Congregations.

98 97 96 95 94 93 92 91   8 7 6 5 4 3 2 1

Text design by Circa 86, Inc.
Illustrations by Allyn Massey

Library of Congress Cataloging-in-Publication Data
Miller, Kenton.
    Trees of life: saving tropical forests and their biological
    wealth/Kenton Miller and Laura Tangley.
        p.   cm.—(WRI guide to the environment)
        Includes bibliographical references and index.
        ISBN 0-8070-8508-1 (cloth).—ISBN 0-8070-8505-7 (pbk.)
        1. Forest conservation—Tropics.   2. Rain forests.
3. Deforestation—Control—Tropics.   4. Forest
policy—Tropics.   5. Forests and forestry—Tropics.
I. Tangley, Laura.   II. Title.   III. Series: World Resources
Institute guide to the environment.
SD414.T76M55   1991
333.75'16'0913—dc20   90-21623
                                                              CIP

CONTENTS

ABOUT WRI GUIDES
TO THE ENVIRONMENT

Every so often there is a sea change in world affairs, and we're amid one now. Environmental concerns are back on the front page and in the nightly news. Even more important, they are being discussed at both the dinner table and the international negotiating table. It has slowly dawned on Americans that waste, pollution, congestion, land degradation, and the like are not isolated mishaps that time will cure but are, instead, by-products of the way we live. And with this recognition has come another: that we have choices to make—the sooner, the better.

We can't make those choices, of course, without a firm fix on the facts and some sense of what's economically and politically possible in our own lifetimes. And we also need a shared understanding of how our busy, productive, big-spending, and still widely emulated country shapes the planet's environmental future, and of how economic and social choices in the rest of the world influence us.

To help Americans grasp the big picture, World Resources Institute created *WRI Guides to the Environment.* These books were written with a sense of urgency to dispel confusion about the greenhouse effect, the loss of rain forests and biological diversity, environment and development in the developing countries, energy and transportation alternatives, and other concerns that newspapers and television usually cover piecemeal or in quick provocative "takes" that leave us either baffled or discouraged. Our belief is that even the most scientifically complex environmental issues can be clearly explained, that there is plenty that all of us can do about them, and that Americans are ready to try.

Kathleen Courrier and Mohamed T. El-Ashry
Series Editors

FOREWORD

Word of rapidly vanishing forests, particularly tropical forests, can't surprise anyone who reads newspapers or watches television. Widespread concern is deepening into conviction, even alarm, and with good reason. Half the world's tropical forests have already been cleared or degraded. Every hour, at least 4,500 acres fall to chain saws, machetes, flames, or bulldozers, and another four plant or animal species die out, most of them in the tropics.

When forests die, so do traditions and livelihoods. In Amazônia, for instance, a thousand peasants, rubber tappers, and other forest dwellers have been killed in the past decade in violent conflicts over forest resources and land. Throughout the tropics, forest-dwelling peoples whose age-old traditions allow them to live in and off the forest without using it to death are losing out to cattle ranching, logging, hydroelectric projects, large-scale farms, mining, and colonization schemes.

Where land is truly well suited to agriculture or other development activities, some forest clearing makes sense. Certainly, not every tree is sacred. But, at current deforestation rates, all but scattered remnants of tropical forest—and a quarter of the earth's species—could be gone before today's preschoolers retire.

The real culprit in this massive assault on nature is rarely the person holding the chain saw or driving the bulldozer or torching the tree that holds up the forest canopy. Looking deeper, it is clear that the fate of the forest is written in population growth, poverty, and the short-sighted policies of governments and international agencies, as well as decisions made by commercial interests and far-away consumers. Some of these policies invite business interests or settlers to convert forests to farms and ranches, or to log or mine or drill for oil. Certain tax incentives support massive projects that transform entire landscapes, and decisions like those on land tenure can make it impossible for poor people to make a decent living without invading ecologically fragile lands. The mighty forces of national debt and international trade imbalances push some developing countries to sell off their forest assets to pay their nations' mounting bills. In industrial countries, commercial logging, especially of the few remaining ancient forests, and pollution also take a toll.

These different kinds of blows to a forest can compound each other. In the tropics, once choice timber has been logged off, the way is open to clear forest land for farming and ranching. As one land use leads to another, species losses accelerate. Forests afire, or felled and decomposing, release gargantuan amounts of carbon dioxide into the atmosphere, amplifying the so-called greenhouse effect and thereby the global warming in store. If habitats are further fragmented while the climate changes during the next century, extinction rates will climb. In industrial countries' forests, pollution thickens the plot: a forest weakened by smog, acid rain, or other airborne ills is more likely to fall prey to insects or disease, not to mention the changed climate forecast for the future.

These facts are painful to recite, but if you are tempted to despair as you read *Trees of Life,* don't. The authors picked an upbeat title for a reason. The loss of forests, species, and cultures at risk isn't inevitable, for there are many things we can do to slow this death rate. What matters most is what governments decide to do, both at home and abroad, for whether forests live or die depends largely on government policies. Tropical nations need to revamp their policies on forestry, agriculture, population, and land tenure. The industrial countries must get serious about controlling pollution and must retool their policies on developing countries' debt, international trade, and aid, including strong initiatives to save America's own old-growth forests.

You can help, too. You can encourage government to keep our forests alive and well and to provide the leadership and funds needed to help conserve tropical forests while making economic development more sustainable and equitable in tropical countries. Closer to home, you can spread the word to friends and family, neighbors and colleagues, helping to build a constituency for rescuing forests and their creatures from extinction.

Fortunately, the steps needed to save forests dovetail with those needed to solve many other nagging problems, from urban smog and acid rain in the United States and other industrial countries to rapid population growth and poverty in the tropics. A particularly compelling reason for acting *now* is that protecting forests will help combat global warming, just as failing to act could invite climate changes more disruptive than those now forecast.

Trees of Life is the second *WRI Guide to the Environment.* (*The Greenhouse Trap: What We're Doing to the Atmosphere and How We Can Slow Global Warming* was the first.) This series was written for people who care about environmental problems and want to get a better grasp of them than the media can deliver but who lack the time or inclination to wade through a carton of technical books. Each guide provides an overview of causes and consequences, scientific findings and uncertainties, and solutions that are as simple as a given topic allows, but no simpler. The next in the series will be a provocative look at why and how transportation and energy use must change if we want to halt greenhouse warming, keep our air breathable, and save the forests and crops damaged by air pollution.

We at World Resources Institute hope that the books in this series will help convert rekindled interest in the environment into personal commitment and public action. Too many sat idly by in the 1980s. The 1990s must be different.

Gus Speth, President
World Resources Institute

ACKNOWLEDGMENTS

Some books are truly group efforts, and this book is one of them. At every stage, the contributions of colleagues, reviewers, and moral supporters made it possible to sustain the momentum needed to make our treatment of such an enormous and important subject timely.

For cooperation and candor, we owe our greatest debt to the staff of the World Resources Institute. Thoughtful reviews by Walt Reid, Tom Fox, James MacKenzie, Robert Repetto, Mark Trexler, Janet Welsh Brown, Robert Winterbottom, Chip Barber, Wilfrido Cruz, and Diana Page turned up errors of both fact and judgment. Hyacinth Billings, Brooks Clapp, and Donna Dwiggins also provided useful comments. Lori Pierelli masterminded production of the book, and Robbie Nichols helped improve its structure and language. Moira Ambrose Connelly lent expert research, writing, production, and editorial assistance from beginning to end. Judith Moore and Lea Borkenhagen brought fresh facts and perspectives to various drafts, and Joe Dever and Tony Zamparutti ably fact-checked several chapters.

Outside of WRI, many people helped us strengthen our case for saving the world's forests and biological diversity. Chief among these are Marc Dourojeanni of the Inter-American Development Bank, Judith Gradwohl of the Smithsonian Institution, Malcolm Gillis of Duke University, Jeff McNeely and Jeff Sayer of the International Union for the Conservation of Nature and Natural Resources, Steve Schwartzman of the Environmental Defense Fund, Kent Redford of the University of Florida, Gordon Orions of the University of Washington, Faith Campbell of the Natural Resources Defense Council, Deanne Urmy of Beacon Press, Susan Gibson Sharpe, and Walter Wells. Deborah Johnson deserves our warmest thanks too.

Inspiration for *Trees of Life* came directly from WRI's president, Gus Speth, a leader in the national and international environmental movement for two momentous decades. His vision and encouragement have been invaluable.

Last, we want to thank Kathleen Courrier and Mohamed T. El-Ashry, the series editors of *WRI Guides to the Environment*. They helped conceptualize this book and forced us to do our best.

K.M. and L.T.

FOREST FACTS

The State of the World's Forests

- *Billions of acres of forest and woodland that have been lost since agriculture began about 10,000 years ago: 2.5*

- *Billions of acres of forest that exist on Earth today: 10*

- *Millions of acres of tropical forest Earth is losing annually: 51*

- *Percentage of Earth's tropical forests that exist in Latin America: 57*

- *Percentage of Earth's tropical forests that exist in Brazil: 30*

- *Percentage of original moist forests remaining in tropical Africa: 40*

- *Percentage of original moist forests remaining in Asia: 37*

- *Portion of U.S. forests cleared between 1630 and 1920: 1/3*

- *Millions of acres of U.S. land that are covered with forest today: 737*

- *Percentage of original U.S. forest area that is tree-covered today, mostly with second-growth forest: 70*

- *Number of acres of old-growth U.S. forests, as of July 1989, that are clear-cut each month: 6,000*

- *Number of minutes it takes a logger with a chain saw to cut down a 33-foot wide, 1,000-year-old tree: 10*

- *Number of acres of old-growth forest that a pair of northern spotted owls, which live only in these forests, need to survive: 5,000*

- *Percentage of U.S. primary, old-growth forests that have been destroyed: 85*

- *Percentage of Madagascar's forests that have already been destroyed: 93*

- *Percentage of Brazil's Atlantic coast forests that have been destroyed: 99*

- *Number of acres of tropical forest that are destroyed each day: 140,000*

- *Number of acres of tropical forest that are destroyed each hour: 5,800*

- *Percentage of the world's tropical forests that were at least somewhat deforested before 1980: 40*

- *Number of different species of trees that have been found in one 4-mile by 4-mile square of Brazilian tropical forest: 750*

- *Number of species of mammals, birds, and reptiles, respectively, found in that same square: 125; 400; 100*

- *Millions of acres of Brazilian rain forest deforested in 1987, a year of intense land clearing by fire: 20*

- *Number of years it will take for all tropical rain forests to be completely cleared if present deforestation rates continue: 177*

- *Percentage of the world's tropical forests that are part of parks and reserves: Less than 5*

- *Ratio of tropical land deforested to tropical land reforested between 1981 and 1985: 10:1*

- *Number of square miles of Central European forest already destroyed or severely damaged, primarily due to air pollution: 23,000*

The State of the World's Species

- *Number of plant and animal species that have been identified and given scientific names: 1,400,000*

- *Millions of plant and animal species that scientists believe exist on Earth: 5 to 30*

- *Percentage of all species that are larger than a bumblebee: 1*

- *Portion of species that are insects or other "spineless creatures": 3/4*

- *Percentage of Earth's plants and animals believed to live in tropical rain forests: 50*

- *How many* more *fish species have been identified in the Amazon River system than in the Mississippi River system: 1,750*

- *Number of ant species that one biologist found in a single tree in Peru: 43*

- *Number of ant species found in the entire British Isles: 43*

- *Number of insect and mite species that live in the fur of a single sloth in Panama: 12*

- *Number of beetle species that live on sloths: 978*

- *Number of wasp species needed to pollinate the world's 900 fig species: 900*

- *Number of wasp species that pollinate each kind of fig: 1*

- *Percentage of Earth's species that could be extinct by the mid-twenty-first century if current deforestation rates continue: 25*

- *Conservatively estimated number of species that are becoming extinct in the tropics* each day: *50 to 150*

- *Number of U.S. plants that face "a real risk of extinction" within five years, according to a recent survey of American botanists: 253*

- *Millions of years that have passed since species extinction rates—based then on natural causes—were as high as they are now: 65*

Our Botanical Dependence

- *Number of plants people use worldwide for food, medicine, and other purposes: 15,000*

- *Out of 75,000 edible plant species on Earth, the number that people have used for food: 5,000*

- *Number of plant species people depend on for 60 percent of their calories and 56 percent of their protein: 3*

- *Billions of dollars that all prescription and nonprescription drugs containing active ingredients derived from plants are worth each year: 40*

- *Percentage of tropical plants that have been screened for medicinal uses: less than 1*

- *Portion of plant species that scientists believe contain compounds with ingredients that are active against cancer: 1 out of 10*

- *Number of tropical forest plants that can possibly offer a cure for cancer: 1,400*

- *Billions of people in the developing world who depend mainly on wood for energy for cooking and heating: 2*

- *Percentage of Earth's population that depends mainly on wood for energy for cooking and heating: 40*

- *Billions of dollars the annual worth of tomatoes increased after a new strain was developed by crossing domestic plants with a wild relative found in South America: 5 to 8*

- *Millions of dollars Florida citrus growers save by using parasitic insects from the tropics to kill citrus-tree pests: 40*

- *Percentage of U.S. gross national product that comes from timber and related products: 4*

- *Millions of tons of paper and board that U.S. citizens consume annually: 69*

- *Percentage that U.S. paper and paperboard consumption increased each year between 1975 and 1984: 3.5*

- *Percentage that the paper and paperboard consumption of Britain and India increased, respectively, per year in the same period: 2.4; 6.6*

- *Billions of dollars that "minor forest products," such as rattan, bamboo, fruits, nuts, and spices, are worth each year: 10*

- *Millions of tons of bananas that people eat each year: 40*

- *Number of tons of mangoes and papayas, respectively, that people eat each year: 1,300,000; 1,500,000*

Side Effects

- *Biggest road-building agency in the world: U.S. Forest Service*

- *Thousands of dollars spent per mile to build a major logging road: 45*

- *Thousands of dollars per mile for secondary logging road: 15*

- *Millions of people who cannot get the fuelwood they need each day, even by overcutting the forests around them: 100*

- *Portion of the developing world's people who will lack a sustainable supply of fuelwood by 2000: 1/2*

- *Number of days a year women and children in some parts of the world spend searching for fuelwood: 100 to 300*

- *Earth's largest exporter of raw wood products: Malaysia*

- *Second-largest exporter of raw wood products: United States*

- *Number of times more money earned by selling fruit, cocoa, and rubber from an Amazonian forest tract than by selling all its trees as timber: 6*

- *Number of times more money earned by selling fruit, cocoa, and rubber from an Amazonian forest tract than by turning it into cattle pasture: 2*

- *Millions of acres damaged annually in India by floods thought to be caused by deforestation of the Himalayan mountains: 12*

- *Number of villages destroyed during India's 1978 monsoon season: 66,000*

- *Number of people evacuated due to deforestation-related flooding in the Philippines in 1981: 331,000*

- *Portion of land in Bangladesh that was under water following similar flooding in 1988: 2/3*

- *Millions of tons of topsoil lost annually on Indonesia's island of Java, which has just 15 percent of its original forest cover: 770*

- *Number of years of service that are regularly lost from hydroelectric dams as a result of sedimentation caused by deforestation: 25 to 50*

- *Billions of tons of carbon dioxide released in 1987 due to forest clearing and other changes in land use: 3*

- *Percentage of annual human-based carbon dioxide emissions that is accounted for by deforestation: 33*

- *Portion of Earth's deforestation-based carbon dioxide emissions that come from Brazil, Indonesia, Colombia, the Ivory Coast, and Thailand: $1/2$*

- *Billions of tons of carbon dioxide that could be absorbed annually by 800,000 square miles of young forest: 1*

1

What Have We Got to Lose?

All over the world, there lingers on the
memory of a giant tree, the primal tree,
rising up from the center of the Earth to the
heavens and ordering the universe around
it. It united the three worlds: its roots
plunged down into subterranean abysses, its
loftiest branches touched the empyrean.
Thanks to the Tree, it became possible to
breathe the air; to all the creatures that then
appeared on Earth it dispensed its fruit,
ripened by the sun and nourished by the
water which it drew from the soil. From the
sky it attracted the lightning from which
man made fire and, beckoning skyward,
where clouds gathered around its crown, it
bade the life-giving rains to fall. The Tree
was the source of all life, and of all
regeneration.

JACQUES BROSSE
The Courier

French naturalist Jacques Brosse's meditation on the ties between
humankind and trees seems a good place to begin a journey into
the forest. If we could plumb deep time, we could trace our
attachment to trees in an unbroken line all the way back to our
prehuman ancestors. The tree is a central image in our cultural
inheritance, radiating its power through the many and various
religions and myths and dreams of our species. Even today's great
monotheistic religions, rooted as they are in the experience of
desert peoples, look on trees as a great good: in Islam, as in the
Judeo-Christian world, the earthly paradise is a garden.

For millennia, this reverence for trees served humankind well.
But now it has faded, and many of the world's remaining forests

are under a virtual death sentence. One-fifth of the 12.5 billion acres of forest that once blanketed Earth are already gone. Each second, more than an acre of tropical forest disappears. Scientific theory suggests that at this rate of forest loss, one species of plant or animal dies out every 15 minutes. If current deforestation rates continue, most accessible tropical forests and up to one-quarter of the earth's species could vanish within the lifetime of today's children.

The developing countries most burdened by debt and rapidly growing populations also have the world's highest rates of deforestation. Certainly, one reason that these struggling nations are under pressure to convert forests into timber and other commodities is the need to fuel economic development, much as Europeans and Americans did during the nineteenth century. The industrial countries owe a good deal of their current wealth to past conversion of forests into towns, farmland, railroad corridors, and fuel for homes and industry—a point not lost on developing countries. Indeed, turning forests into something that seems more immediately useful has been a hallmark of Western civilization (and most other cultures) from the beginning. Greece, once heavily forested, was already a naked peninsula by the end of the fifth century B.C., when Athens was in its glory. Greek forests lived on in myth, but in reality they had been converted into the myriad ships of a seagoing power.

In the past, though, forests' recovery odds were better than they are now because the human population was relatively small, technologies for forest clearing were unsophisticated, and the forests under siege were mostly in temperate zones, not the tropics. Relatively speaking, temperate forests are hardy and resilient, and will spring back if they are left alone, largely because up to 97 percent of the nutrients required for new forest growth are stored in the soils. In contrast, tropical forests store up to 90 percent of their vital nutrients in the vegetation that is removed in whole or part during deforestation.

In any case, until the last century or two the world was sparsely populated enough that temperate or tropical forest areas altered in the name of small-scale agriculture, timber harvesting, or fuelwood collection often recovered on their own. But now the burgeoning human population is demanding a constant flow of food, building materials, fuelwood, minerals, energy, and other valued items so great that nature's ability to provide them indefinitely is in question. And now the conditions favoring forest regeneration—loose, reasonably fertile soils; seed sources from nearby forest stands; diverse species of pollinating and seed-dispersing birds, insects, and mammals; and freedom from recurrent fires, pollution, and other disturbances—can't be taken for granted.

How are we to become better stewards of our domain so that we can pass on to future generations a world on the mend, rather than one broken and impoverished? A quantum leap in knowledge and a transformation in values seem necessary, an almost revolutionary change in how we view nature.

Eating the fruit of the tree of knowledge brought our first parents to grief in their garden paradise, according to the ancient story. Moderns might argue that the Fall was an evolutionary leap into consciousness and power, but, unfortunately, our power has outrun our foresight. Our knowledge has allowed us to flourish as a species, but our very success now threatens to ruin us.

According to Genesis, naming the animals in the Garden of Eden was one way in which humanity asserted dominion over all other creatures. Sadly, many species are now dying nameless, and names may soon be all that is left of others, thanks to human misrule. If we are to save what is left of nature, our understanding of good and evil must come to include what we do to the earth. If we can manage that sort of leap, we may right our balance with nature and at the same time finally earn the name *Homo sapiens* we so immodestly gave to ourselves.

TAKING STOCK

Historically, nations in the temperate zones have cleared forests with a will. The United States, which had nearly 950 million acres of forest when the Pilgrims arrived in Massachusetts, is no exception. Colonists spreading up and down the eastern seaboard, pioneers and ranchers and railroaders pushing westward, and other early Americans felled forests to make way for towns, farms, ranches—whatever the local economy needed. Much of the timber cut during the nineteenth century was used as fuelwood or charcoal to fuel the American industrial revolution. By 1920, more than a third of the vast forests that were standing in the seventeenth century had vanished. Had deforestation continued at that clip, the year 2000 might have found the United States all but treeless. But that didn't happen. Instead, as in most industrial countries, rural people streamed into cities and towns, and most forests began to recover. On the Atlantic coast, in the Appalachian mountains, and in a few other areas, forest cover increased because abandoned farmlands were left to return to forest. From 1964 to 1986, however, the United States cleared 1,140 square miles of forest to again make way for urban and suburban growth, including its ever-expanding network of highways.

In the tropics, where soils are poor, forest recovery can be painfully slow. When a tropical forest is cut down, life-giving nitrogen, phosphorous, and other plant nutrients may initially be flushed into the soil, but rain soon washes them away. Once the trees are gone, the land rapidly becomes infertile. Within three or four seasons, crops fail, and colonists have no choice but to move on and turn a new tract of forest into cropland.

This progression from forest to crops to crop failures is all too common throughout the tropics, but it is not inevitable. Indigenous gardens have long flourished in the Peruvian Amazon and the Mayan regions of Mexico and Central America. Indonesians have kept their traditional rice-irrigation systems going for generations. The record leaves no doubt that local communities can produce food, medicine, building materials, and fuelwood for centuries on the same sites, especially if crops are rotated. In some modern adaptations of these age-old methods, pasture and fruit, timber, or fuelwood trees are mixed or layered, and vegetables are grown among the trees. By imitating the wild and even husbanding the local insect population, farmers can produce crops without relying on mineral fertilizers or pesticides. As researchers at Rodale and Winrock Institutes and North Carolina State University at Raleigh have demonstrated, a combination of organic fertilizers, mixed cropping, crop rotation, and "minimum tillage" techniques can regenerate and maintain agricultural productivity indefinitely in both temperate and tropical areas.

Still, when large expanses are cleared, tropical forests may rally only very slowly, if at all. Depleted soils aren't the only obstacle to recovery. Most tropical trees are pollinated by birds, insects, and other animals, often by just one or a few species. If deforestation wipes out these pollinator species by destroying their habitats, the few surviving trees cannot reproduce. Animals and birds also spread trees' seeds, so if they perish when forests are cleared—as many do—seeds don't get dispersed. Even if a tenacious seed does manage to sprout, a tropical tree seedling is notoriously sensitive to any change in temperature, humidity, and light, and only certain pioneering species can grow in open or cleared land.

If the clearing of tropical forests is limited to small patches like those around traditional villages and farms, pollinators and seed carriers can still do their job, and the forest may survive. The impact of temperature, humidity, and light along the edges of small clearings isn't very harsh either, so the forest can make a quick comeback, especially if the soil has not been trampled by livestock or otherwise abused. Chances for recovery are worse where the forest has been destroyed by small-scale gold-mining operations, which now number in the hundreds of thousands in the Amazon region alone. Bulldozers and dredgers deforest stream banks and surrounding lands, leaving a landscape reminiscent of wartime bomb craters. The sterile upturned rocks make it doubly difficult to control erosion, and gashes in the land discourage pollinators and seed growth. The upshot is extra decades of recovery time for the battered forests.

However sensitive they are to assault, tropical forests hold great biological riches. They cover just 7 percent of the world's land area but contain at least half of all plant and animal species. These species, most of which exist only in one or another forested region, are at the same risk as their habitats. Scientists believe that countless numbers have already died out in the wake of tropical deforestation. Prospects for the future are even grimmer, as people convert and burn more forests.

WHAT'S A TREE WORTH TO THE AVERAGE URBAN AMERICAN?

Exactly what are privacy, shade, bird-nesting sites, and a welcome break from asphalt worth anyway? The value of some forest uses is difficult to calculate in dollars. But some efforts along these lines have been attempted. According to the American Forestry Association (AFA), the United States' 70 million or so acres of urban tree spaces are worth more than $50 billion. As for a single tree, in 1985 AFA's Gary Moll estimated that an average 50-year-old city tree would provide $73 worth of air conditioning, $75 worth of erosion and storm water control, $75 in wildlife shelter, and $50 in air pollution control in one year. Adding a little for inflation, Moll calculated the worth of a single urban tree over its half-century lifetime at $57,151.

Assessments like these aren't lost on real estate agents. Property with trees commands higher prices than property without them, all other things being equal. Older, larger trees are prized most, but, according to the U.S. Forest Service, suburban homeowners can boost property values by up to 20 percent—an average increase of $3,000—by adding trees to their lot.

Growing concern about the greenhouse effect and global warming may also increase the value of trees. Because trees shade buildings, they decrease the need for air conditioning, which decreases the use of electricity, much of which is derived from fossil fuels—main sources of greenhouse gases that contribute to global warming. AFA estimates that planting more trees in cities could shave $4 billion a year from national energy costs. Even three strategically placed trees around a house can cut home air conditioning costs by from 10 to 50 percent.

In principle, logging doesn't have to damage the forest's capacity to regenerate. But all too often timber is harvested carelessly. Typically, only large valuable trees are felled. The young seedlings and saplings waiting patiently on the forest floor for a place in the sun are uprooted and left to die. Branches, crowns, and stumps—which account for half a tree's total mass—are left scattered around the quarter-acre patch that remains when a mammoth tropical tree is felled. The remains of the cut trees and damaged understory dry out in the sunlight—one reason the cut forest burns so easily.

What is the way out? How can we stop killing forests and their denizens—and stop damaging our atmosphere in the bargain? Surprisingly, the answer takes us far afield from what most of us think of as forestry. To begin with, we must find ways to relieve the widespread poverty, demographic pressure, and hunger so rampant in the tropics. Granted, forests also fall so that wealthy corporations may turn a profit and some of us may buy rosewood furniture or throwaway packing crates. But in much of the tropical world, the most relentless pressure on the forest comes directly from long-held custom or government policies. Where laws allow the wealthy few to own or control access to most of the best land, the many who are poor can't find productive employment or the space needed to grow food or use forest lands wisely with the long term in mind. Where governments promote forest clearing for cattle ranching and development schemes largely to generate foreign exchange, the effect is often to reinforce landlessness, poverty, and hunger. Similarly, government's failure to clamp down on illegal gold mining in the Amazon leads to ecological and social destruction and the loss of economic assets that could support development. In these and many other cases, it's government policy that drives the poor deeper and deeper into the forest to find food for their families and eke out a living.

The legitimate aspirations of the poor, the inequitable distribution of fertile cropland, and the designs of corporations, ranchers, and wealthy consumers might in sum be more than enough to threaten tropical forests' demise. But the last straw may turn out to be runaway population growth and migration into the regions where forests are most at risk. Human need is now increasing exponentially, while the size of the forest left to meet it dwindles. It doesn't take a math genius or a disciple of Thomas Malthus to see that both people and forests will suffer mightily in the coming crunch, unless something gives soon.

THE RETREATING FOREST

How fast are tropical forests disappearing? Until recently, the most authoritative figure—29 million acres per year—was from a 1980 study conducted by the United Nations Food and Agriculture Organization (FAO). By the mid-1980s, says FAO, tropical closed forests (that is, those in which tree tops form a canopy) were being *cleared* for agriculture or other purposes at the rate of about 18.5 million acres per year. Another 11 million acres or so were being *logged* but not cleared. More current information, however, based partly on satellite surveys and new definitions of deforestation, indicates that deforestation in Brazil, Costa Rica, India, Myanmar (formerly Burma), the Philippines, and Vietnam is worse than previously thought. Clearing is also more severe than expected in Cameroon, Indonesia, and Thailand. If new studies are accurate, Earth is losing up to 51 million acres of tropical forest per year—a 79 percent increase over the losses calculated in 1980.

Recent studies summarized in *World Resources 1990–91* show deforestation rates generally rising. In the 1990s, we can expect clearing and logging on up to 40 million of the existing 4.2 billion acres of tropical forestland per year—that's roughly 110,000 acres each day, or 170 square miles—an area about the size of Chicago.

Exactly how fast tropical forests are disappearing has been hotly debated for years, and until we know the answer, it will be hard to convince decision makers of the problem's importance. Monitoring trends and setting priorities for inventorying, protecting, and managing forests will involve some guesswork. Present estimates range wildly. FAO and other UN agencies hope to finish a new forest inventory by 1991, but even that won't be comprehensive enough to fill the knowledge gap. What we need to complete the picture is solid local and regional data.

There are several ways to gather this sort of information. For accuracy, you can't beat a surveyor who is actually there on the scene measuring the amount of forest cover, but this method requires prodigious amounts of labor, money, and time, so it's used mainly for small samples. At the other extreme are high-tech

methods: remote-sensing equipment on high-flying aircraft and
satellites can piece together a complete panorama of worldwide
forest cover. Today's weather satellites already record some data
from each continent every day. The trouble is that, although satellite systems now in use regularly measure deforestation in such
key areas as the Brazilian Amazon, only paltry sums have been
invested in the broader global effort.

Since groping in the dark is no longer an option, and since
the tools for the job exist, many scientists are up in arms that
governments are doing so little. Many researchers want an all-out
global assessment of forest cover and deforestation using satellite-
based remote sensing, work that could be done for as little as $5
million a year in the initial phase—about what Americans spend
on salted snack foods *every four hours*. The idea is to combine
the inexpensive, low-resolution images taken by weather satellites
with costlier high-resolution images taken in key areas by other
satellite systems, such as Landsat. Random ground-level checks
could round out the picture.

Perhaps the growing popular political support for saving tropical
forests will spur governments to cooperate. But unless that happens soon, it won't matter. Time is running out. As NASA scientist
Compton Tucker told *Science* magazine, "many people are talking
about the importance of quantifying deforestation, but nobody is
actually doing the work. It's pathetic. Let's face it, in another 10
years, it won't be worth doing."

Regional "snapshots" are especially needed. Global deforestation rates can be misleading, because the amount, kind, and
causes of decline vary so much from place to place. Tropical
moist forests have been disappearing eight times faster in Costa
Rica, the Ivory Coast, and Nigeria than the global average
suggests. Brazil, too, far exceeds the average. In 1987, satellite
images of the Amazon Basin captured the destruction of 20
million acres.

The normally hardy forests in the United States and other tem-
perate-zone nations can't be taken for granted either. In recent
years, the pattern of forest decline in the United States, Europe,
and Canada has matched the spread of acid rain and other airborne
pollutants. Pollution-weakened trees make perfect targets for

pests and disease. The extensive damage that tiny pear thrips wreaked on New England's sugar maples in 1988 makes the point: the trees were ripe for disaster because they had already been bathed in acid rain. Indeed, tens of thousands of acres of once-healthy forest in North America and Europe are now in critical condition, thanks largely to acid rain and other air pollutants.

THE GREENHOUSE CONNECTION

The atmospheric consequences of large-scale forest loss are two-fold. First, there is the release of carbon dioxide, nitrous oxide, and methane into the atmosphere, where they intensify the natural greenhouse effect and contribute to future global warming. Second, deforestation reduces the forests' capacity to absorb carbon from the air, an important regulatory mechanism in the natural carbon cycle.

The theory that certain gases warm a planet's atmosphere was first laid out by French mathematician Jean Fourier more than 150 years ago. After sunlight strikes Earth's surface, some of it is radiated back into space as infrared energy. The so-called greenhouse gases—carbon dioxide, methane, chlorofluorocarbons, nitrous oxide, and ozone—slow the escape of this infrared energy into space, thus warming the atmosphere. Indeed, the heat trapped by naturally occurring greenhouse gases is what keeps Earth's average temperature warm enough to suit us. But our closest neighbors, Venus and Mars, illustrate the fire-and-ice possibilities of this process. Venus, with a dense atmosphere composed largely of carbon dioxide, has a runaway greenhouse effect and a surface temperature hot enough to melt lead. Mars, with a thin atmosphere low in greenhouse gases, has a surface temperature of − 76 degrees Fahrenheit!

Earth, fortunately, is in the mid-range, but concentrations of greenhouse gases have risen dramatically, thanks to human activity, threatening to turn the natural greenhouse *effect* into a greenhouse *problem*. The leading culprit is carbon dioxide: more than four-fifths of this century's 25 percent increase in atmospheric carbon dioxide can be traced to fossil fuel burning since the Industrial Revolution began. (Global commercial energy production now emits almost 7.3 billion tons of carbon annually, and deforestation adds another 3.1 billion tons a year.) Forests and forest soils contain 20 to 100 times more carbon per acre than do pastures or croplands. When forests are burned to prepare cropland, an immense storehouse of carbon built up over decades or centuries surges into the atmosphere. Forests that are felled or flooded and left to rot release great quantities of methane, and this gas is (on a molecule-for-molecule basis) 70 times as powerful as carbon dioxide at trapping heat. In all, deforestation accounts for nearly one-fifth of the global warming that's in store—and its contribution is rising.

Uncertainties about how fast forests are disappearing and how much carbon different kinds of forest contain make accurate estimates of the net release of carbon from tropical deforestation difficult. But there is no doubt that a good bit of the buildup of greenhouse gases comes from deforestation. According to *World Resources 1990–91,* Brazil emitted about nine tons of carbon dioxide per capita in 1987, mostly through deforestation, including fire. In other words, Brazilians released nearly twice as much carbon per capita into the atmosphere through deforestation as Americans did by burning fossil fuels and making cement. Bear in mind, though, that the United States is still the world's leading producer of carbon dioxide: Americans make up a mere 5 percent of world population but produce over 17 percent of all greenhouse gases (mainly as industrial and transportation emissions).

Just as Fourier's theory predicts, the global average temperature has risen by about 1 degree Fahrenheit over the past century. Most scientists now believe that greenhouse gases already banked in the atmosphere commit Earth to a global average temperature increase of from 1 to 2 degrees Fahrenheit by sometime in the next century. Temperature increases and their consequences in the middle latitudes, where nations such as the United States lie, will be greater than the global average, while equatorial regions will experience far less change. The as-yet-unknown time it takes to spread heat absorbed by the atmosphere throughout the system, mainly the oceans, makes for a time lag between today's temperatures and an inevitably warmer future. Another degree or two may not sound like much, but it is enough to disrupt both human and natural systems, to change climate and weather, to raise sea levels the world over, and to make species hard-pressed to adapt. And it won't necessarily stop at 1 or 2 more degrees. If current rates of emission and deforestation hold steady for another four decades, by the year 2030 we could be committed to an average global temperature increase of from 3 to 8 degrees Fahrenheit. For that matter, the rise will not stop until some decades *after* we stop changing the atmosphere's composition.

DELUGE

In most tropical regions, rainfall is abundant but erratic: wet and dry seasons are as distinct as night and day, and when the rains come, they can be torrential. Forests cushion the effects of sudden downpours by intercepting part of the rain, which then evaporates and so returns to the atmosphere. Forests also blunt the force of a deluge as raindrops fall gradually from leaf to leaf through successive layers of the canopy. This means that much of the rain that eventually reaches the ground will be captured by soil and organic litter and released slowly to plants and streams and rivers. Deforested regions have no such effective raintraps.

British environmental expert Norman Myers calls such trapping "the sponge effect." As long as "forest cover remains intact," he writes in *The Primary Source,* "rivers not only run clear and clean, they flow throughout the year. When the forest is cleared, rivers start to turn muddy, then swollen or shrunken." According to Myers, an undisturbed forest in Southeast Asia intercepts at least 35 percent of all rainfall; some 65 percent of the rain reaching the soil nourishes plants or enters streams as groundwater. In contrast, a partially logged forest in this tropical region intercepts less than 20 percent, and a tree plantation of rubber or palm trees planted in rows captures only about 12 percent. In a violent deluge, logged forests and tree plantations let through so much water that soil erosion and flooding are common.

Thanks to the sponge effect, intact tropical forests protect the watersheds that support 40 percent of all farmers in developing countries. For that matter, a big share of the 340 billion gallons of water that Americans use daily also comes from forested watersheds. Unfortunately, in recent years many vital watersheds in developing countries have been cleared, sometimes with devastating results. When deforestation upsets natural water systems, disastrous floods can alternate with equally disastrous droughts.

The irrigated Asian lands that produce nearly one-third of the world's food supply have already been hurt by such all-or-nothing cycles in deforestation's wake. In Thailand, Indonesia, the Philippines, and other Asian ricebaskets, farmers can no longer count on getting enough irrigation water when they need it. Periodically, water shortages bring enormous hardship: heavily deforested peninsular Malaysia lost well over a quarter of its rice harvest back in 1977–78—a loss estimated at about $95 million.

On the other side of the coin, 331,000 people had to be evacuated in 1981 in the Philippines because of flooding. Damage to crops, livestock, and buildings totalled $30 million. After the flood, then-President Marcos declared deforestation a national emergency. Eight years later, a similar crisis hit Thailand. In 1989, the Thai government banned logging throughout the country after heavy flooding wreaked havoc throughout the nation's densely populated lowlands.

SILT AND MUD

Fierce tropical rains not only unleash floods but also carry off topsoil—two menaces that healthy forests temper. The awesome force of a tropical rainstorm makes protection against it essential. In the many tropical countries where rainfall exceeds 120 inches a year, a 30-minute storm can dump 2 inches of rain, up to 40 times as much as delivered by an average shower in New England. Water rushing down deforested slopes carries off soil by the ton, leaving the land too impoverished to grow crops or generate new forest.

Soil erosion has reached calamitous proportions in many tropical nations. In the Cauca Valley watershed in Colombia, 20 tons of soil per acre were lost from the deforested slopes in just ten months. Cropland in Madagascar, which was once almost completely covered with tropical forests, loses up to 130 tons of soil per acre each year. Nepal each year loses up to 36 tons of soil per acre. The densely populated Indonesian island of Java has only 15 percent of its original forest left and annually loses about 770 million tons of topsoil from its croplands.

Errant topsoil can be particularly menacing to hydroelectric projects because it silts up the reservoirs. Throughout the tropics, dams have lost years to deforestation and subsequent soil erosion. In the Philippines, the Ambuklao Dam—built to last 56 years—is now expected to be silted up in just 32. In Pakistan, the Mangla Dam has lost about 50 of its 100 years of potential service; and in Costa Rica sedimentation of the Cachi Dam will cost at least $133 to $274 million in lost revenues. In the Dominican Republic, which spends up to 80 percent of the income it earns from exports on hydropower development, erosion rates of up to 270 tons per acre—50 times the losses in the U.S. breadbasket—are threatening the longevity of many dams.

In the most ill-fated hydropower projects, reservoirs silt up even before the waterworks are fully built. China's Laoting Reservoir filled with sediment before the dam was finished, forcing workers to abandon the project. Ironically, a plant's construction often contains the seeds of its destruction. Typically, the hundreds or thousands of construction workers brought in are forced to forage for their own shelter, food, and fuelwood. As a result, the area around the dam site is stripped of forest cover by the time the reservoir's fill-up date arrives. Lands "opened up" this way also become prime settlement areas. Once they are occupied, erosion intensifies and more soil tumbles into the reservoir, reducing its storage capacity and clogging the electric generator's turbines.

Silt also jams shipping canals. In Panama, for example, the average annual deforestation rate during the 1980s was 140 square miles a year. At this rate, virtually all the country's watersheds above the Panama Canal could lose their forest cover and seriously erode by 2000. As early as 1977, sedimentation and drought together had already brought water levels in the canal so low that some cargo ships had to be diverted around Cape Horn—an expensive 11,615-mile detour!

Topsoil isn't good for fish either. Several fishing grounds off the Philippines coast are declining as a result of sedimentation caused by deforestation. Because the Philippines now exports $100 million worth of oysters, mussels, clams, and cockles, this loss of productivity could be very expensive.

CULTURES FELLED WITH THE FOREST

The specter of cultural extinction hangs over hundreds of thousands of tribal people who live in the forests of Africa, Asia, and Latin America. "All these people, who live entirely in and off the forest, are the only ones who have mastered the art of exploiting the rain forests on a really sustained basis, thanks to an enormous amount of practical knowledge," writes Marius Jacobs in *The Tropical Rain Forest*. "They know everything about food plants, medicinal species, edible insects and their larvae, and the collection of wild honey. With bow and arrow or a blowpipe they hunt the scarce animals of the rain forest to obtain protein." Tragically, the people most threatened by deforestation are the very people who know things about living in harmony with nature that their countrymen competing for space in the forests need to learn.

In Chiapas, Mexico, about 450 Lacandón Maya Indians still live in their traditional way in North America's largest remaining tropical rain forest. Until the 1960s, the Lacandón Maya were virtually isolated from outsiders, so they have preserved their way of life far longer than have other Mayan groups. Logging roads constructed in 1965, however, abruptly ended this isolation and sovereignty. Hundreds of thousands of colonists and cattle ranchers streamed into the forest, threatening both Lacandón traditions and the forests themselves.

Today, more than half of the Lacandón rain forest is gone. But the small group of Lacondón Maya who remain in the region still practice a form of ecologically sound agriculture passed down from generation to generation for many centuries. This agroforestry system combines tree crops with food and other crops. Masters of this system can produce up to 79 kinds of food and fiber products simultaneously and keep the same plots productive for up to seven years in a row, compared to the one or two growing seasons that nearby colonists usually get. Even after seven years, rubber, cacao (the basis for cocoa and chocolate), citrus, and other easy-care trees are planted. Eventually, the plots are allowed to return to forest and left to recover for several years before being cleared to begin the cycle anew.

Indigenous groups living throughout the rest of Latin America, Asia, and Africa are also ecologically savvy. In Thailand, the Lua harvest more than 200 wild plant species for food and other purposes. These people are also consummate land-use planners: they designate different categories of forest around their villages and declare some off limits to farmers and wood collectors. In Zaire, the Efe pygmies of the Ituri Forest gather more than 100 species of forest plants to eat and to make tools, baskets, dyes, and medicines. For some months of each year, the Efe dine exclusively on forest plants and animals.

Worldwide, tropical deforestation has decimated the indigenous groups that depend on forests for their survival. Their tribal lands fall prey to colonists, miners, and loggers and the people themselves to violence, or, more likely, disease. Measles and influenza carried into the forest by colonists kill people who have never before been exposed. Even if they escape with their lives, indigenous peoples are being forced to give up their traditional cultures. Many tropical countries—if they have any government policy at all toward forest dwellers—have one designed to take them out of their forest homelands and absorb them into the dominant culture.

The loss of traditional rain forest cultures is the world's loss, for they know how to relate to nature in a symbiotic rather than parasitic way—wisdom that the world sorely needs. As Susanna Hecht and Alexander Cockburn put it in *The Fate of the Forest,* "this knowledge [on the part of indigenous and local populations] permits an understanding of the forest as the outcome of human as well as biological history, and hence the view that humans can continue to make their history in the forest, sustaining and sustained."

HOTBEDS OF EXTINCTION

Apart from the loss of human life and ways of life, the most catastrophic result of tropical deforestation may be the mass extinction of hundreds of thousands, perhaps millions, of plant and animal species. Most biologists agree that we are already amid an extinction crisis unmatched in at least 65 million years and that, if current trends continue, one-fourth of the world's species may be headed for extinction in the next 25 to 50 years.

What will such losses mean to those of us who live in temperate zones? Ethically, they will stand as a devastating critique of our excessive consumption, "fast" life styles, and misguided development approaches and economic arrangements with tropical countries. Unless we change, we ourselves will have to say goodbye to many products and environmental services that we daily take for granted, and our children will inherit a harsher, stingier world and a narrower set of options for feeding, housing, and clothing themselves, staying healthy, and adapting to a changing environment.

As the fate of many North American songbirds attests, some of these options have already been lost. Bird-watchers have noticed a trend that soon may hit even the most indifferent citybred observer: there aren't nearly as many songbirds around as there were 20 years ago. Tanagers, orioles, warblers, and hummingbirds are among the migratory populations that have declined precipitously, hard hit by forest loss in Central and South America, where they spend the winter. Nearly two-thirds of the birds that summer in North America winter in Latin America or the Caribbean, so many populations are at risk. If this decline continues, the loss will not be merely aesthetic—fewer songs ringing out in the early morning, fewer splashes of color at the birdfeeder. It will also take a toll on our food supply and forests, since some of these migrants eat mosquitoes, worms, caterpillars, and other voracious insects that ravage crops and northern forest trees, while other songbirds pollinate plants and spread seeds.

How fast are the world's plants and animals disappearing? Even experts have to guess because nobody knows how many species call Earth home. So far, about 1.4 million species have been named and described—some 250,000 flowering plants, 750,000 insects, and 41,000 vertebrates. Yet, except perhaps for vertebrates and flowering plants, the catalogue of life forms is far from complete. "Remarkably," states Harvard biologist

E. O. Wilson in *Biodiversity*, "we do not know the true number of species on Earth, even to the nearest order of magnitude." Wilson's highly educated guess is that the number falls somewhere between 5 and 30 million.

At least half the species catalogued so far live in moist tropical forests. "The species diversity of rain forests borders on the legendary," writes Wilson. "Every tropical biologist has a favorite example to offer." His own: "From a single leguminous tree in the Tambopata Reserve of Peru, I recently recovered 43 species of ants belonging to 26 genera, about equal to the entire ant fauna of the British Isles."

Another Harvard scientist, Peter Ashton, identified 700 tree species in ten 2.5-acre plots in Borneo. On 2.5 acres in the upper Amazon, Alwyn H. Gentry of the Missouri Botanical Garden found up to 300 tree species. At one site, almost two-thirds of the trees were the only member of their species present: of the first 50 trees sampled, only 2 were the same species. Gentry believes these Amazonian forests may be the world's richest in tree species.

As amazing as these head counts are, the biological wealth of tropical forests can't be calculated simply by ticking off lists of species. Tropical forests also contain a high proportion of species that are found nowhere else in the world. These so-called locally endemic flora and fauna tend to develop in isolated areas where populations of the same species have been separated from each other—sometimes for eons—by water, mountains, or other geographic barriers. If enough time passes, these isolated populations adapt to differing local conditions and finally evolve into different species. For this reason, islands are havens of locally endemic species.

In a temperate forest, more than half of all trees may be of the same species. But in a tropical forest of about the same size, a single species may account for only 5 to 10 percent of the total. Unfortunately, small populations are at tremendous risk when their habitats get carved up. As small groups get broken into even smaller ones, extinction at the hand of predators, competitors, pests, disease, or bad weather becomes more likely. Then, too,

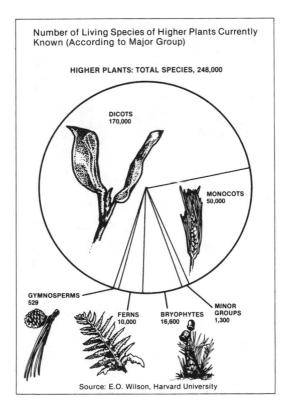

Number of Living Species of Higher Plants Currently Known (According to Major Group)

HIGHER PLANTS: TOTAL SPECIES, 248,000

DICOTS
170,000

MONOCOTS
50,000

GYMNOSPERMS
529

FERNS
10,000

BRYOPHYTES
16,600

MINOR
GROUPS
1,300

Source: E.O. Wilson, Harvard University

the extinction of a single species of plant, bird, bat, or rodent could lead to the extinction of other species that depend on it for pollination, seed dispersal, food, or defense. In a worst-case scenario for creatures that reproduce sexually, a population could shrink so much that chance variation could leave it entirely male or entirely female. Even if it avoids this certain route to oblivion, any small population is at risk. It's hard to find suitable mates in a small pool of candidates, and some species can't mate unless they have plenty of company. (Birds of paradise, can't mate, for instance, unless a throng of males first assembles and "struts its

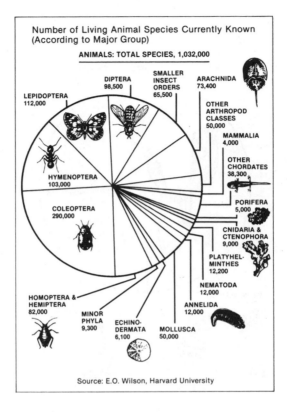

Number of Living Animal Species Currently Known
(According to Major Group)

ANIMALS: TOTAL SPECIES, 1,032,000

LEPIDOPTERA
112,000

DIPTERA
98,500

SMALLER
INSECT
ORDERS
65,500

ARACHNIDA
73,400

OTHER
ARTHROPOD
CLASSES
50,000

MAMMALIA
4,000

OTHER
CHORDATES
38,300

HYMENOPTERA
103,000

COLEOPTERA
290,000

PORIFERA
5,000

CNIDARIA &
CTENOPHORA
9,000

PLATYHEL-
MINTHES
12,200

NEMATODA
12,000

HOMOPTERA &
HEMIPTERA
82,000

ANNELIDA
12,000

MINOR
PHYLA
9,300

ECHINO-
DERMATA
6,100

MOLLUSCA
50,000

Source: E.O. Wilson, Harvard University

stuff'' in front of the females.) Even if a few hardy or lucky
survivors defy whatever risks they face, inbreeding may gradually
make them unable to adapt to environmental changes.

How serious are the die-outs in tropical forests expected to be?
For the last two decades or so, scientists have used the observed
relationship between the size of a forest tract and the number of
species found in it to estimate losses in species richness. Ecologist
Walter Reid of the World Resources Institute estimates that by
the year 2020 up to 17 percent of species living in the tropical
forests of Asia, Africa, and South America may vanish unless
today's deforestation rate drops. If it doubles, Asian tropical for-

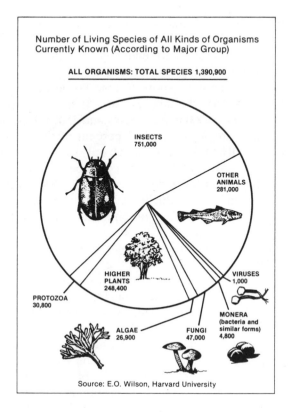

Number of Living Species of All Kinds of Organisms
Currently Known (According to Major Group)

ALL ORGANISMS: TOTAL SPECIES 1,390,900

INSECTS
751,000

OTHER
ANIMALS
281,000

HIGHER
PLANTS
248,400

VIRUSES
1,000

PROTOZOA
30,800

ALGAE
26,900

FUNGI
47,000

MONERA
(bacteria and
similar forms)
4,800

Source: E.O. Wilson, Harvard University

ests could lose close to half their species. If one-fourth of *all* species vanish by 2050 or so, as some scientists predict, and if we assume (very conservatively) that Earth houses 10 million species, 15,000 to 50,000 species are dying out each year in the tropics. That's 50 to 150 species per day!

As bad as this sounds, some experts claim that the situation is even worse in certain areas. According to ecologist Norman Myers, extinctions could soon be exceptionally high in ten tropical forest regions: Madagascar, the Atlantic coast of Brazil, western Ecuador, the Colombian Chocó, the uplands of western Amazônia, the eastern Himalayas, peninsular Malaysia, northern

Borneo, the Philippines, and New Caledonia. These "hotspots," says Myers, contain 34,000 plant species and at least 700,000 animal species that are locally endemic, and their deforestation rates are higher than the global average.

Myers expects these hotspots to lose 90 percent of their remaining forests within the next decade. If they do, we can bid farewell to roughly 17,000 plant species and 350,000 species in all. In this rash of extinctions, nearly 7 percent of Earth's plant and animal species will be lost, even though only 0.2 percent of Earth's land area is involved. And the losses could be even greater. Since Myers first pinpointed these hotspots in 1988, his pessimism has deepened. In at least two of the hotspots—western Amazônia and the eastern Himalayas—deforestation's spread is even faster than he had anticipated.

Although extinction is a natural part of life and evolution, we are today wiping out plant and animal species 1,000 to 10,000 times faster than before the human species came along. Myers calls this "extinction spasm" the "greatest single setback to life's abundance and diversity since the first flickerings of life almost 4 billion years ago."

In both size and kind, today's extinction crisis differs from extinction episodes of the past. According to E. O. Wilson, a more or less steady "background" rate of extinction has been interrupted five times—roughly, at 26-million-year intervals—by "major extinction episodes." Although millions of species may have died during these mass extinctions, in none were extinctions spread throughout all major categories of species, as they are today. For example, most mammals, birds, amphibians, and many reptiles survived the late Cretaceous extinctions 65 million years ago that did in the dinosaurs. Most plants survived *all five* mass extinctions, but today this hardy kingdom is shrinking rapidly.

Even worse in terms of the long-term prospects for diverse life forms on Earth is the loss of entire ecosystems today—coral reefs, wetlands, and estuaries, as well as tropical forests. According to Myers, these environments were long "powerhouses of evolution" and gave rise to many more species than other environments did. After the mass extinction episode at the end of the Cretaceous

Era, it took from 5 to 10 million years for a similarly diverse group of species to evolve. During the current interglacial period—the past 12,000 years—Earth has been richer in species than at any other period in its long history. With human beings now wiping out whole categories of plants and animals, as well as entire ecosystems, recovery this time will certainly take much longer. Some ecosystems may *never* recover as long as human activities continue unbridled. As a result, we may witness what Wilson has called "the death of birth."

NATURE'S PHARMACOPOEIA

Some species extinctions will be particularly painful for *Homo sapiens*. Tropical rain forests, with their dizzying array of plants and animals, offer the promise of new medical treatments for age-old and newfound human ills. Most of the natural compounds used in medicines come from toxins that plants produce to keep from being eaten. Tropical forests boast an incredible arsenal of these defensive chemicals because they are home to more species of plants and plant predators than any other ecosystem. To date, the potential medical benefits of this vast genetic storehouse have scarcely been tapped. Less than 1 percent of tropical plant species have been screened for medical applications, but even that tiny sample has yielded enormous benefits.

As an example, consider the profound impact of the rosy periwinkle on two life-threatening diseases. This tropical dry-forest plant from Madagascar has greatly increased the survival odds of the thousands of people who suffer from Hodgkin's disease and childhood leukemia. Thanks largely to drugs derived from this plant, leukemia victims now have a 99 percent chance of remission and Hodgkin's disease sufferers a 70 percent chance. Thirty years ago, only one in five childhood leukemia victims recovered, and a diagnosis of Hodgkin's disease nearly always meant imminent death.

Other major drugs in the tropical plant lineage are also impressive. Tubocurarine, made from the South American vine *Chondodendron tomentosum,* is widely used as a muscle relaxant during surgery. The heart medicine ouabain is derived from a West African vine, *Strophanthus gratus*. The antimalaria drug quinine is made by boiling the bark of cinchona trees. More than 260 South American plants appear to have potential fertility control applications. Of the 3,000 plants identified by the National Cancer Institute as having anticancer properties, 70 percent live only in the tropics.

The possibilities for developing still more new drugs from tropical forests should figure heavily in any calculation of the forest's true worth. All 119 plant-derived drugs used worldwide today came from fewer than 90 of the 250,000 plant species that have been identified. Each such plant is a unique chemical factory, says Norman R. Farnsworth of the University of Illinois at Chicago, "capable of synthesizing unlimited numbers of highly complex and unusual chemical substances whose structures could [otherwise] escape the imagination . . . forever." In other words, scientists may be able to synthesize these plant compounds in the laboratory, but dreaming them up, rather than plucking them from the forest and then replicating them, is quite another matter.

How much money is this effort worth? For the past 25 years, says Farnsworth, one-fourth of all prescription drugs dispensed from American pharmacies contained active ingredients derived from flowering plants. Commercially, these plant-derived medicines are worth about $14 billion a year in the United States and $40 billion worldwide. In 1985, Lilly Research Laboratories sold roughly $100 million worth of vincristine and vinblastine—the periwinkle derivatives used to treat childhood leukemia and Hodgkin's disease—and turned a stunning 88 percent profit.

Surprisingly, U.S. pharmaceutical companies do very little research on developing new drugs from wild plants. Why? For one thing, the industry has come to rely more on synthesized chemicals than on natural compounds for drugs, so the backlog of active natural substances still waiting to be tested is growing. For another, drug companies worry about whether they will be able to patent uses of natural products. The U.S. National Cancer Institute, on the other hand, recently earmarked $8 million to screen 50,000 natural substances for activity against 100 cancer cell lines and the AIDS virus. China, Germany, India, and Japan, among others, are also screening wild species for new drugs.

Forest peoples originally discovered the medicinal uses of three-quarters of the plant-derived drugs currently in wide use. In the northwestern Amazon, indigenous people use at least 1,300 plant species to create *drogas do certão* or "wilderness drugs." In Southeast Asia, traditional healers use 6,500 different plants to treat malaria, stomach ulcers, syphilis, and other disorders. The World Health Organization estimates that 80 percent of people in the developing world rely on traditional medicine based largely on the use of medicinal plants.

THE FOREST AS AN ECOSYSTEM

Without so-called ecosystem services, Earth would be uninhabitable to people and most other animals. We need plants to convert sunlight into usable energy, and we need nature's billions of tiny unsung decomposers—primarily insects, fungi, and microorganisms—to keep us from drowning in our own wastes. Indeed, an estimated 95 percent of the 6 billion tons of organic waste generated by Americans each year is degraded by organisms, while only 5 percent is burned. Plants and animals also help cycle carbon, nitrogen, oxygen, sulfur, and phosphorus, all of which are essential to life. In the United States each year, some 154 million tons of nitrogen are sapped from the soil by crops. Nitrogen-fixing organisms return about two-thirds of this lost nitrogen fertilizer to the soil. And, as we have seen, forests temper droughts, flooding, and the flow of water to farms, factories, and homes.

Without forests and other natural ecosystems, these cycles would unravel, forcing our children to wrestle with survival issues that we barely have to think about. But at what point do ecosystems—none of which has totally escaped the imprint of human handiwork—stop providing the essential ecological services people need to survive? Unfortunately, we probably won't know the answer until it's too late to avoid the damage. Considering this uncertainty, and the drastic consequences of losing these basic functions, the conservative approach would be to keep as many natural systems together and whole as we can. Aldo Leopold said it best in *Sand Country Almanac* in 1949: "If the biota, in the course of aeons, has built something we like but do not understand, then who but a fool would discard seemingly useless parts? To keep every cog and wheel is the first precaution of intelligent tinkering.''

Our tinkering so far has been less than intelligent, and certainly less than enlightened. But the good news is that with a change of heart and ways we can still save most of the enterprise. All is definitely not lost.

2

A Short History of Assaults

The major problems in the world are the
result of the difference between the way
nature works and the way man thinks.
GREGORY BATESON, 1976

How protective we feel about forests depends partly on whether we recognize the enormous evolutionary debt we owe to plants, a debt that reaches deep into the past. Without an event that took place more than 3 billion years ago—the rise of the first organisms that convert sunlight into usable energy through photosynthesis—life on Earth might have been completely different.

Before these ancestors of modern plants arose, Earth's first primitive organisms lived solely off organic compounds formed from atmospheric gases over millions of years. The first photosynthesizers came along in the nick of time, for this source of food was beginning to run out. Photosynthesis not only sustained life but also changed its course by changing the atmosphere. By splitting water into hydrogen and oxygen, these plant ancestors released oxygen into the atmosphere, where it now makes up about one of every five molecules. Soon after, another form of oxygen—ozone—began accumulating in the outer atmosphere, where it blocks out some of the sun's deadly ultraviolet rays. Thanks to stratospheric ozone, living things once restricted to the deep sea began to flourish at the water's surface and, ultimately, on land.

Plants themselves made their evolutionary debut about 430 million years ago when green algae invaded the land. During their first 100 million years or so, plants took on diverse forms but remained relatively small. Then, competing for light, they evolved into taller and taller forms; by roughly 300 million years ago, abundant and diverse forests graced every land mass. For 250 million years, these long-lived giant plants ruled the natural world. But when climate changes began creating deserts, savannas, grasslands, and the rest of today's familiar landscapes, forests started to shrink.

When human beings first started driving animals with fire some 200,000 years ago, a new phase of accelerated forest loss began. One can imagine these fires burning out of control, slowly changing the forest, creating more prairies and savannas. Some 10,000 years ago, with the dawn of agriculture, the pace of deforestation quickened as people cleared land for fields and grazing. It slipped into high gear in temperate zones during the eighteenth and nineteenth centuries when more land was cleared to grow food for expanding industrial-based cities and to meet spiraling demand for construction timber and fuelwood. Clearing of tropical forests began in earnest in the 1950s.

Around the world, different forests face different threats. In the tropics, wholesale clearing of tree cover is the main issue, though so-called selective logging is causing growing problems, too. In the United States, Europe, and most other temperate regions, the chief concerns are air pollution, the logging of old-growth stands, and the loss of woods along rivers and in remnants of other types of forests.

In most places, both deforestation and forest degradation stem from human intervention and natural processes that influence each other. Which factors in which degrees and combinations bring on deforestation in a particular area is a question as complicated as whether nurture or nature makes us who we are. Rarely does a forest come undone because of a single event, be it a swath cut by a bulldozer or an act of God. Usually, repeated disturbances or several kinds of disturbances are to blame. To take one example, if settlers fragment a forest, humidity and temperatures within the remaining forest change, making it more susceptible to fire and to plant and animal losses. Rainfall can decrease or shift seasons. The migratory birds and insects needed for pollination and seed dispersal can take history-making detours. If the forest is also feeling the effects of acid rain, climate change, or freak storms, the damages can be crippling.

Add to this somber scenario the diverse pressures of economic development—logging, ranching, mining, building roads and dams, farming, gathering fuelwood—and it's easy to see why

---

DEFINITIONS

Sixty seconds' worth of technical definitions can make it easier to grasp the threats to forests. The word *deforestation* itself means different things to different people. The authors of *World Resources 1990–91* define it as "the permanent clearing of forest lands for use in shifting cultivation, permanent agriculture, or settlements." Forest *degradation* refers to damage or loss of quality, whether from air pollution and the harvesting of old-growth trees in temperate zones or from selective logging, extensive grazing, "slash and burn" agriculture, and small-scale mining in the tropics. Some writers use the term *deforestation* more loosely to cover both the clearing and the degradation of forest lands, but in this book, *deforestation* means full-scale conversion or loss of forest and *degradation* means significant alteration, but not loss.

---

experts can disagree on exactly what dooms a particular forest. Still, they know only too well the main ingredients of forest degradation and collapse.

TIMBER!

Tropical forests provide about one-fifth of all the wood used worldwide in industry, and, as wealthy nations turn increasingly to the tropics to satisfy their seemingly insatiable hunger for wood, that share is expected to grow. Today, tropical forests supply about 30 percent of the world's log exports, about 12 percent of sawnwood exports, and about 60 percent of plywood and veneer exports. In the 1990s, the UN Food and Agriculture Organization (FAO) expects that about 53 billion cubic feet of wood will be consumed each year, largely by industrial nations. Leaving fuelwood aside, that's about 10 cubic feet per person worldwide. By the year 2000, total world consumption will rise to 64 billion cubic feet.

In recent years, global demand for tropical hardwoods (mostly in the form of unprocessed logs) has soared. Prized for their strength and varied colors, these hardwoods also resist decay and termites. Finding an American home today that does not contain furniture, plywood, veneer, wood siding, salad bowls, or some other familiar item that was once part of a tree in Southeast Asia or the Amazon would be difficult. And cheap wood products, such as the rough forms for concrete pouring used in construction, are industrial mainstays. Small wonder, as the National Academy of Sciences reports, that hardwood imports by industrial nations are 15 times higher than they were in 1950!

The largest single consumer of tropical hardwoods today is Japan. Its roughly 124 million citizens account for nearly one-third of the entire international market—more tropical wood than Belgium, Denmark, France, West Germany, Greece, Ireland, Italy, Luxembourg, Netherlands, Portugal, Spain, and the United Kingdom use together. With two-thirds of its land covered with forests that provide wood products and protect watersheds, soils, scenery, and wildlife, Japan itself is now more heavily forested than any other industrial nation except Finland. Since World War II, when it lost its forestlands in Manchuria and Sakhalin Island, it has bought wood abroad as a way to protect its own forests.

Close behind Japan in use of the world's tropical hardwoods is the United States. Here, too, demand for hardwoods has been outstripping growth in population and gross national product. Together, production cost hikes and national regulations that control logging for conservation's sake have driven up the prices of forest products in the United States, making it "economically rational" to import plywood and veneer from Southeast Asia through suppliers in Japan, South Korea, and Taiwan. Americans now buy 70 percent of all tropical plywood and veneer that enters the world market.

A few more statistics put the U.S. role into perspective. Between 1950 and 1973, U.S. imports of tropical hardwoods increased ninefold. The National Academy of Sciences expects them to double again by the year 2000. These imports satisfy only 2 percent of this country's total wood demand; in 1987, the average American used about 57 pounds of imported lumber. But they contribute in a big way to the overexploitation of Southeast Asia's dwindling tropical forests.

The tropical wood destined for the United States travels along a few south-to-north routes. Most comes from Southeast Asia, mainly Indonesia, Malaysia, and the Philippines. According to Malcolm Gillis of Duke University, tropical Asian countries supplied five-sixths of the volume of global tropical hardwood exports in the mid-1980s. In 1982, says Gillis, Malaysia and Indonesia each exported more tropical hardwood products than all Latin American and African countries combined. Peter Ashton of Harvard University says that Southeast Asia now supplies nearly two-thirds of *all* kinds of timber in international trade. But Southeast Asia's share of the international timber market will fall sharply if the region's forests continue declining.

That fall seems inevitable. Developing countries desperately need foreign exchange, and to get it they are logging their forests far faster than nature can renew them. Fears of new restrictions on logging, including international agreements and boycotts, have intensified pressures on some forests. Logging companies in Malaysia, for instance, have recently turned harvesting into a 24-hour-a-day operation, working under lights at night! Logging at such a furious pace obviously can't go on much longer. Several countries have already lost timber markets they once had, and only 10 of the 33 nations that now export tropical hardwoods are expected to be in the export business by the year 2000.

As Asia's forests disappear, pressure on Africa's and, especially, Latin America's forests will increase. But by how much? A computer model developed by the Oxford Forest Institute has one answer. The Asian-Pacific countries that now supply more than 80 percent of all tropical hardwood exports will supply just 10 percent a decade from now.

When timber exports fall in deforestation's wake, an important source of revenue goes with them. Unfortunately, government policies in many exporting nations invite this double whammy. In most timber-rich tropical nations, governments own most of the forests but sell logging rights to corporations, many of them based overseas. To maximize profits, these corporations look mostly for high-value timber species, which they ship to Europe, Japan, and elsewhere for processing. Under this arrangement, the harvesters and processors make most of the money to be made, not the owners of the forest.

Regardless of whether foreigners or wealthy landowners control forest concessions, overexploitation results. Just as renters care less than owners do about what happens to a piece of real estate, concessionaires lose no sleep over the long-term fate of the forest if they have only short-term contracts with governments.

So far, more than 500 million acres of tropical forest have been logged. Currently, another 10 million acres are commercially logged each year. Little of the acreage controlled by commercial loggers is technically "clear cut." But "selective" logging—the removal of, say, one to four high-value logs per acre—can easily degrade the remaining forest.

The bitter truth is that, although selective logging *can* be carried out efficiently, with little damage to the surrounding forest, it rarely is. Timber companies usually harvest the biggest and tallest trees. When those giants topple, they pull down or injure dozens of their neighbors, some of which are connected to "the target tree" by a tangle of vines. According to forest expert Norman Myers, a typical selective logging operation in Southeast Asia "injures beyond repair" one-third to two-thirds of all trees in the stand. "Hence," Myers says, "the cynic's account of how a typical corporation practices selective logging: it selects a forest, and then logs it."

SACRED COWS?

In the last 45 years, large tracts of Latin America's forests have been partitioned into huge plantations where rubber, palm oil, cocoa, coffee, tea, sugarcane, bananas, and other export crops are grown. More recently, still more forestland has been cleared to make way for pastures for cattle.

Some of the rough-and-ready charm conferred on cattle ranching by cowboy movies still clings to the enterprise. But its role in the destruction of Latin American forests, particularly in Central America and the Brazilian Amazon, is anything but glamorous. Between 1950 and 1975, Central America's pastureland more than doubled—most of it carved out of virgin forest. The number of beef cattle also more than doubled to at least 9 million. Today,

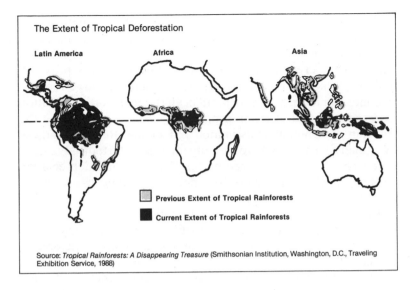

The Extent of Tropical Deforestation

Latin America   Africa   Asia

☐ Previous Extent of Tropical Rainforests

■ Current Extent of Tropical Rainforests

Source: *Tropical Rainforests: A Disappearing Treasure* (Smithsonian Institution, Washington, D.C., Traveling Exhibition Service, 1988)

over two-thirds of all Central America's farmland is devoted to cattle ranching.

Few of these ranches last much longer than do new farms carved out of the forest. After 10 or 15 years at best, most are abandoned for greener pastures. Like virtually all former rain forest lands, these pastures quickly lose their fertility. They also become easy targets for erosion, fire, and invasion by weeds that are toxic to cattle. If ranchers burn their fields, the nutrient-rich ash will keep them at least marginally productive for a while, but before long these pastures cease producing enough edible grass to support a money-making venture. Many ranches in the Brazilian Amazon last only 5 years. Writer Catherine Caufield claims that nearly all the ranches established in the Amazon before 1978 had been abandoned by 1985 and were too beaten down by cattle hooves and overburned to produce anything except rough scrub. "The pattern of clearing, repeated burnings, falling productivity, and abandonment is now familiar to ranchers," says Caufield.

Obviously, such short-lived commercial ventures have not produced the profits expected by their backers. But some Brazilian ranchers have made fortunes even while their ranches went broke, thanks to tax credits, subsidies, and other incentives provided until very recently by the government. Some 470 large ranches accounted for more than 20 percent of all Brazilian forest alteration observed by Landsat monitoring up to 1980—while costing the Brazilian government an estimated $2.5 billion. Returns on these investments went straight to wealthy ranchers who took advantage of generous tax credits, income-tax holidays, and depreciation allowances, while writing off the ranches' operating losses against taxes due on income from other sources.

Despite this abysmal record, international organizations and development agencies continue to back cattle ranching in the tropics. According to the U.S. Office of Technology Assessment, between 1971 and 1977, these agencies gave more than $3.5 billion in loans and technical assistance to improve livestock production and meat processing in Latin America. By 1983, the World Bank alone spent about the same amount on livestock just in Latin America.

Why did cattle ranching boom in Latin America? Culture plays a part. With roots in Spain and Portugal, ranching has long been considered a prestigious occupation throughout the region, and it often pays better than farming. Also, though cattle ranches may come and go, they last longer and cost less to start up than commercial crop production. Yet, the driving forces behind the boom have been larger.

To shore up the economies of fledgling democracies, governments and international lenders turned to the few surefire commodities that could be counted on to sell well in international markets and earn the foreign exchange needed to help revive the economy and pay off debts. In Central America, that meant pushing production of coffee, bananas, and, especially, cattle. As Sheldon Annis of the Overseas Development Council reports, between 1969 and 1985, roughly one-third of all state-financed agricultural credit ($1.2 billion) went to cattle production.

Unfortunately, cattle production didn't even pay back the loans, much less turn the profit that had been expected. Even so, according to Annis, as recently as 1987, credit for cattle ranching was eight times that for the production of such economic mainstays as ornamental plants, macadamia, melon, root crops, tobacco, reforestation and irrigation works, and other traditional areas of agricultural investment combined. Even the bottom line couldn't change investment policy, never mind the threat of deforestation.

By 1982, Americans were eating some 53 billion pounds of beef annually. Of this, less than 3 percent was imported, and most imports came from Australia and New Zealand. But, while less than 0.5 percent—about 330 million pounds a year—came from lands that were once Latin American tropical forests, the Central American forests still felt the impact. How could it be otherwise when the United States was buying 25 percent of Central America's annual beef production and 90 percent of its beef exports?

With cheaper beef now available elsewhere, the United States has recently cut back on beef imports from Central America. But cattle ranching continues to be a major cause of deforestation because Central American urbanites are now eating more and more beef, and the U.S. contribution to the problem still has some conservationists worried.

Although Americans claim to be diet conscious, most find grass-fed beef too lean, so nearly all Central American beef imports are mixed with domestic cattle trimmings before they wind up as hamburgers, hot dogs, processed meats, or pet food. Convinced of a "hamburger connection" to tropical deforestation, some U.S. conservationists have supported boycotts of major fast-food chains, with varying degrees of success. Yet, it's almost impossible to make the case that a particular chain imports Central American beef. Once the U.S. government inspects beef imports, the meat enters the domestic market without any labels showing where it came from. Some of the largest chains claim they don't use any foreign beef, and conservationists have no way of proving that they do—if they do.

Not everyone agrees on the role of beef production in deforestation, however, or in the effectiveness of boycotts. Is the forest simply cleared acre by acre by small-time farmers trying to make a living from whatever crop pays best? Or do governments and banks deliberately promote cattle ranching on forestland that then has to be cleared? Writing in the journal *Oikos*, tropical biologist Daniel Janzen of the University of Pennsylvania claims that a forest is cleared "to grow people, not a specific crop and only that crop. If the market does not buy a crop, then the forest clearing will be used for a different crop." Still, most evidence suggests that, in Costa Rica and elsewhere, agricultural policies invite ranchers with medium-sized to large holdings to expand their pastures and open up lands at the expense of the tropical forest.

Critics of boycotts also believe that eliminating markets for a tropical nation's export crops hurts these countries and does nothing to protect their tropical forests. Wouldn't it be far better, they say, to get governments to offer incentives and set prices that reflect how much it really costs the country's people and environment to produce crops, beef, and other products on once-forested land? For example, prices for timber products, beef, minerals, and electrical power could be raised enough to cover the full cost of managing and protecting the forest area and reforesting or restoring sites where habitats have been degraded. In this way, people would have an incentive to take greater care in handling valuable resources, and government agencies, private companies, farmers, and communities would have a compelling reason to keep long-term environmental quality and economic security in mind. Those who ignored these powerful signals might go broke.

BLOCKBUSTER DEVELOPMENT

Many millions of acres of forest have fallen in the name of progress and modernization. Hydroelectric dams, roads, oil-production facilities, mines, cash-crop plantations, and population resettlement schemes have knifed into previously impenetrable forests, paving the way for further incursions, both planned and spontaneous. While the goals of these projects—producing crops or energy, developing markets, creating jobs, integrating various parts of a country, or shoring up national security—may be noble in the abstract, their actual effects on people and natural resources are quite controversial. Some experts say that too few of the benefits of blockbuster development touch the lives of the poor. Others decry the widespread forest destruction that accompanies these enormous projects.

Some megadevelopments in Brazil (covered in the next chapter) have spelled environmental disaster and made headlines around the world. Most of the fuss has been over projects initiated to settle and develop the vast Amazon Basin at the expense of the rain forest and the native peoples who were once the region's only human inhabitants. As in other countries, many of these ill-fated megaprojects have been financed with loans from the World Bank and other international financial institutions.

Indonesia's transmigration program also exemplifies block-buster development. The Indonesian archipelago, encompassing more than 14,000 islands, suffers from an extreme imbalance in population distribution. The fertile "inner islands" of Java and Bali make up only 7 percent of the land but house two-thirds of the country's 170 million people and produce two-thirds of the nation's food. By contrast, the vast, mostly forested "outer islands" of Sumatra, Borneo, Sulawesi, and New Guinea are sparsely populated. Governments since the Dutch colonial rulers early in this century have dreamed and schemed about ways to transfer "excess" population to the outer islands, and uncounted numbers of upwardly mobile Javanese have made the move on their own as well. But since mid-century, resettlement's pace has quickened. Between 1950 and 1979, some 828,000 transmigrants made the move under government sponsorship, and official transmigration rapidly picked up steam with the infusion of over $500 million in World Bank loans between 1976 and 1986. Between 1979 and 1986, nearly 1.5 million people took advantage of the program to migrate, making it the world's largest government-sponsored resettlement program. In a country where the 1987 per capita share of gross national product was only $450, an estimated average of $6,000 per family was spent on relocation.

While some transmigrant settlements have prospered, many have not. The reasons vary: some settlers were not farmers to begin with, and some of the land is just too poor or arid to produce for anyone. The construction of houses, market roads, schools, drinking water systems, and the like has often been substandard and years overdue. Seeds, farm tools, and fertilizers often arrive after the planting season, and squabbles over who owns title to the land discourage settlers from putting in the hard labor needed to build a farm from scratch. Widespread corruption, incompetence, and bureaucratic indifference make matters worse.

Just as many immigrants to the United States in the nineteenth century moved west looking for a better life, Java's landless poor are drawn to the outer islands by the hope of economic opportunities. Indeed, migration and settlement seem inevitable. But on what terms? Certainly, the current model is flawed. In some settlements, 30 percent of the transmigrants are abandoning their plots to look for work in nearby towns or to return to Java. Meanwhile, as the International Institute for Environment and Development concluded in 1985, transmigration has harmed forests more than any other economic activity. Charles Secrett of Friends of the Earth estimated in 1986 that "80 percent of the transmigration sites to be set up during Indonesia's current Five Year Plan [1984–89] will be hacked out of untouched jungle. The result will be the overall loss of at least 3.3 million hectares [7.44 million acres] of some of the richest rainforest in the world." Figures from the World Bank are substantially lower but still represent what it calls "an important loss of tropical rain forest."

For the last five years or so, Indonesia's government has defended transmigration as a way to strengthen national borders and increase national security. Even so, since 1986 both the government and the World Bank have cut back support for new settlements. Now the government has its hands full trying to regulate people who migrate spontaneously, whose numbers dwarf those of officially sponsored migrants. As the emphasis switches to schools and other basics in eight large settlements, what will the fate of the forests be? Important lessons have been learned in Indonesia, but the springboard for future destruction is in place. The roads and settlements provide the access and staging ground for tomorrow's assaults on the forest, and the failure of many farms and towns has ignited the search for new, temporarily more fertile plots and for such forest products as wildlife and rubber.

With poverty and urban congestion threatening minimal living standards and even life in many tropical countries, economic development of some kind is a necessity. But on what terms will the world's remaining tropical forests be thrown into the bargain?

FARMING THE FOREST

In some parts of the world, carving farms out of the forest is often a two-step affair. First come the loggers. Then colonists follow logging roads into the forest, cutting down the unsalable trees left behind. There, they plant crops, build homes, and try to make a better life. According to the UN Food and Agriculture Organization, half or more of logged forests will eventually be cleared by land-hungry farmers, each of whom clears just enough for his family to survive.

Alan Durning of the Worldwatch Institute recently visited a once-landless family that now farms in a small clearing of what had been virgin rain forest. Roman Barriga's farm lies about six hours by rutted dirt road from Santa Cruz, Bolivia. Barriga, who had struggled for 15 years as a day laborer on a big ranch in the country's Valle Seco region, "where we could never get ahead of the debts we owed to the landlords," told Durning: "Four years ago, I made up my mind to try my luck out here in the forest." His voice quickened. "The first year, I cut the trees and burned them. And the corn grew tall and sweet in the ashes, and we all thought we had finally made it. What a party we had!"

According to the National Academy of Sciences, in the mid-1970s, some 140 million farmers like Roman Barriga occupied roughly 772,000 square miles of the world's tropical forest. These and the farmers who have since joined their ranks are now clearing at least 38,600 square miles a year. As for the future, the tremendous population growth that has taken place in tropical nations in recent years has probably thrown even worst-case projections off.

The rural populations of most tropical nations are the fastest growing on Earth, and the good arable land in many of these countries (especially in Latin America) is controlled by a powerful, privileged few who grow export crops rather than food crops for local use. Often, the poor wind up in the rain forests simply because they have nowhere else to go. Like foot soldiers in a war of attrition, these farmers are buffeted by forces and decisions beyond their control.

Roman Barriga and countless other tropical forest settlers get good yields from their new farms for one or, at the most, a few years. But after uprooting their families and traveling hundreds, even thousands, of miles, these families struggle with disease and the other dangers of the forest only to have their farms fail. So, no sooner have they settled in one new place than they must pick up and move again, clearing new land and beginning the tragic cycle anew.

As mentioned in Chapter 1, new farms carved out of old forest fail mainly because most tropical soils don't have the nutrients needed to sustain crops, and farmers don't have the money to buy fertilizers to replace these nutrients. But does this mean that forests should be off limits for agriculture? Not necessarily.

Tropical forests have been farmed successfully by longtime forest residents for thousands of years. So-called shifting cultivation (also called "swidden" or "slash-and-burn" agriculture) has flourished throughout the tropics. "Shifting cultivation is known as *caingin* in the Philippines, *chena* in Ceylon, *conuco* in Venezuela, *ladang* in Malaysia and Indonesia, *milpa* in Central America, and *roça* in Brazil, to name but a few terms," writes Marius Jacobs in *The Tropical Rain Forest*. "Throughout the tropics the methods are essentially the same." Shifting cultivators first carefully pick a small plot of land. They then clear away all trees and other vegetation and set the trees afire. Ash from the burned wood fertilizes the soil so that a mixture of crops, such as corn, potatoes, rice, and cassava, can be grown for 2 or 3 years. When the soil loses its fertility, the farmers move on to a new plot, letting the exhausted one recuperate for from 15 to 30 years. When they return, the land is restored enough to farm again. With enough land and not too many farmers, shifting cultivation is ecologically sound in the tropics. In Southeast Asia, shifting cultivation has been the number one form of agriculture since at least 1000 B.C. There and elsewhere, it has sustained tropical forest dwellers without destroying their forests. Such prosperity is possible, however, only where plots are abandoned for a decade or more between rounds of cultivation and where fire used to help clear small sites is carefully controlled.

Even where there is land aplenty, this system requires great skill and knowledge. A family of shifting cultivators may be simultaneously working up to 30 plots in various stages of cultivation and abandonment! One such family, observed in Peru by Christine Padoch of the New York Botanical Garden's Institute of Economic Botany, grows several crops (including combinations of rice, plantains, papaya, corn, manioc, tomatoes, green peppers, coriander, watermelon, and cowpeas) in each plot and also tends fruit orchards kept in various stages of cultivation and fallow. "As fruit trees pass their prime yielding state, as some get too tall to harvest easily, and as other, newer orchards begin to yield, less time and management is usually devoted to the field," writes Padoch. As the family withdraws its attention and its demands, "the orchard soon comes to resemble a young forest more than an agricultural undertaking."

Drawing on accumulated knowledge and ancient tradition, shifting cultivators make the most of what nature has given them. Indeed, as Catherine Caufield writes in *In the Rainforest,* "the more 'primitive' a farming system is, the more knowledgeable and skillful the farmer must be. Shifting cultivators . . . traditionally create in their fields a partial replica of the complexity of the forest, its diversity, its several layers, its mixture of plants and animals." Often, shifting cultivation is the *only* way that food, fodder, and fiber can be wrested from the fragile soils of tropical forest ecosystems.

But now these ancient farming systems are breaking down. The impact of roads, ranching, colonization, rapid population growth, and the aftermath of logging—especially fires—are forcing ever larger numbers of shifting cultivators to return to plots that have not been allowed enough time to rest and recover. Land this worn out is quickly degraded and abandoned.

Increasingly, these traditional farmers have been joined by hundreds of thousands of new forest migrants who, like Roman Barriga, have been pushed into this last frontier. Few come to the forest possessing the experienced shifting cultivator's precise, handed-down knowledge of the soil and lay of the land,

and pioneers' ignorance of tropical forests often costs them
dearly. After one productive season, Roman Barriga's new farm
seemed to turn on him. "Since then, things have gone bad,"
he told Alan Durning. "The soil gets drier, and it won't grow
anything but weeds. I tell you, the weeds here never sleep. And
the pests? I've never seen so many kinds. My wife and daughters
had to go to the city to look for work . . . as domestics, as
washerwomen, because the corn won't grow right. We're just
about done for." Says Durning: "Tens of millions of peasants
who have gone into the rain forests in hopes of a better future
could have told the same sad tale."

FUEL FOR THE FIRE

Remember the "energy crisis" the United States faced in the
1970s? Imagine that, instead of waiting in long lines and paying
higher prices at the gas pump, we had to spend up to 300 days a
year scouring the countryside for enough fuel to cook our meals
and heat our homes. That is exactly the sort of energy crisis faced
by millions of people in tropical nations today. For them, the
question is not how they can limit the number of miles they drive
or the amount of electricity their household gadgets consume, but
how they can cook food or keep warm.

Today, more than two-thirds of the people in poor countries
depend on wood to get through the day. In most African nations,
wood provides nearly two-thirds of all household energy. Unfortunately, in many areas where fuelwood is needed most, it is getting
harder to find. In the early 1980s, about half of the 2 billion people
who depend on wood and other traditional fuels for cooking and
heating could not find enough wood. The other half had to overex-
ploit wood sources to make ends meet.

In all, two out of every three developing nations are in the
throes of severe fuelwood shortages. Hardest hit are western
Africa—particularly south of the Sahara—and parts of Asia. Most
of these nations can't afford alternative sources of energy, and
FAO predicts that, by this century's end, nearly 3 billion people
won't have enough fuelwood to get by.

The endless search for wood dominates the lives of millions of

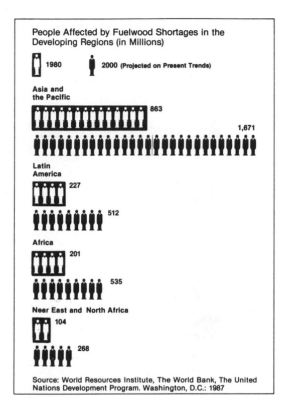

People Affected by Fuelwood Shortages in the Developing Regions (in Millions)

1980   2000 (Projected on Present Trends)

Asia and the Pacific
863
1,671

Latin America
227
512

Africa
201
535

Near East and North Africa
104
268

Source: World Resources Institute, The World Bank, The United Nations Development Program. Washington, D.C.: 1987

people—mainly women, who traditionally are saddled with the job of collecting wood and finding water. As wood supplies dwindle, this sometimes daily search takes women farther and farther from home and robs them of time they could spend tending crops, preparing food, caring for children, learning new skills, and starting new enterprises.

When all wood supplies within walking distance finally give out, weary wood gatherers turn to substitutes. Usually, the only ones on hand are crop residues and animal dung—surprisingly precious materials that would otherwise be used to fertilize fields. The cost of this switch is high. Each year, burning roughly 400 million tons

Fuelwood's Share of Total Energy Consumption, 1982

DEVELOPED COUNTRIES
1%

DEVELOPING COUNTRIES
26%

LATIN AMERICA
20%

AFRICA
52%

ASIA
22%

Source: World Resources Institute, The World Bank, The United Nations Development Program. Washington, D.C.: 1987

of dung as fuel reduces grain harvests by more than 14 million tons—nearly twice the annual amount given worldwide as food aid. "For many families, it costs as much to heat the supper bowl as to fill it," writes Norman Myers in *The Primary Source*. When substitutes are gone, the cost becomes higher still: families switch to less nutritious, faster-cooking foods or eat uncooked meals. Eventually, malnutrition follows and, if there is no fuel for boiling water, disease.

Although dead wood burns better, wood foragers sometimes have no choice but to cut live trees—a hard blow to the forest. In southern Mexico and parts of Central America, for instance, wood gathering has taken an immense toll. Recently, writer Jim Conrad spent several days with a family in Amatenango del Valle in southern Mexico. Returning after one day-long firewood search with Máximo, the family's son, Conrad tried to reconcile his remorse for the region's battered forests with his recognition that Máximo's family has no other choice:

> At least five other choppers can be heard working at various locations nearby; five people with axes gnawing at the forest, day after day, year after year, generation after generation. . . . A brown-backed solitaire sings its exquisite bubbling, tinkling song, and for a moment I feel a kind of anger. Soon the firewood gatherers will convert the solitaire's forest—what is left of it—into low scrub and pasture. . . . But then I recall Máximo's family sing-talking [by] the fireplace that morning, and I ask myself just what such a family is to do without firewood when the morning is cold and tortillas need to be made.

What indeed?

AIR POLLUTION: A GROWING THREAT TO FORESTS

Accidents of birth have spared most of us who live in the temperate zones the kind of suffering associated with tropical deforestation. But today many temperate forests are in deep trouble, and recent evidence suggests that one blight that is hurting them is cropping up in tropical forests, too.

Throughout the United States and Europe, trees are falling sick and dying. In some places, weird deformities jar even casual observers. In others, natural pests that were once only a nuisance are wiping out large stands of weakened trees. Mystified for years by these phenomena, scientists now generally agree that acid rain and air pollution play a leading role, if not *the* leading role, in temperate forest decline.

Ailing forests first commanded public attention in Germany in the late 1970s. Silver fir in the famed Black Forest were losing needles and then dying in large numbers. Norway spruce was the next species to show signs of disease, followed by pine, and then hardwoods in 1982. According to James MacKenzie and Mohamed T. El-Ashry, authors of *Ill Winds: Airborne Pollution's Toll on Trees and Crops,* "discoloration and premature leaf fall have now been reported for essentially all major forest tree species in West Germany." Although tree damage first showed up only at elevations above 2,500 feet, it has now spread to lower elevations as well. Germans have named the phenomenon *"neuartige Waldschaeden,"* or "new type of forest damage."

By 1980, *Waldschaeden* had spread throughout Central Europe, killing trees growing at all elevations and on all types of soil. According to MacKenzie and El-Ashry, since the early 1980s about 23,000 acres of Central European forests have been damaged. "In Europe, scientists generally agree that air pollutants number among the primary causes of forest decline," they report. "No other factor can explain the near-synchronous decline of so many different species over so vast an area." In the United States, tree loss and damage have afflicted every region for at least 25 years. So far, mortality rates are highest in California, though large numbers of trees have also sickened and died high in the Appalachian Mountains from North Carolina to Maine.

Damage to California's pines and other conifers was initially noticed in the 1950s in the San Bernardino Forest, about 75 miles east of Los Angeles. Hardest hit have been ponderosa and Jeffrey pines; 1969 surveys showed 100,000 to 160,000 acres with moderate to severe damage. Later surveys revealed similar problems in the Laguna Mountains, the Sierra Nevada, the San Gabriel Mountains, and Sequoia National Forest, with damage increasing over time. "While slightly under half of all surveyed trees showed some injury in 1980–82," say MacKenzie and El-Ashry, "85 percent did by 1985." What is the principal culprit? Recent research indicates that it's excessive amounts of ozone. Curiously, while ozone is essential in the upper atmosphere for filtering harmful ultraviolet rays, at ground level it is a serious air pollution problem. Ozone damages plant tissues, inhibits photosynthesis, and increases plants' susceptibility to disease, drought, and other air pollutants.

In eastern North America, red spruce trees have taken the worst beating. For about 30 years, these commercially valuable trees have been turning brown and dying on mountaintops up and down the East Coast. Many that survive look yellow and stunted. Scientists monitoring patches of forest throughout the region have found that one-fifth of the red spruce alive in 1982 had died by 1987—a mortality rate about eight times that of trees at lower elevations. While air pollution seems to concentrate at higher elevations, trees farther down the slopes are also beginning to show telltale signs of injury.

This damage is easy to spot. Writing in *Natural History*, University of Vermont botanist Hubert W. Vogelmann described a red spruce forest in Vermont's Green Mountains: "Gray skeletons of trees, their branches devoid of needles, are everywhere in the forest. Trees young and old are dead, and most of those still alive bear brown needles and have unhealthy looking crowns. . . . As more and more trees die and are blown down, the survivors have less protection from the wind, and even they are toppled over. The forest looks as if it has been struck by a hurricane."

Just what causes forest decline in the United States and Europe has bedeviled researchers, because many factors—acting singly and in concert—are involved. Complicating things further is the difficulty of replicating natural conditions in an experiment. So far, most of the evidence linking air pollution to tree death has come from the laboratory, where experiments show how pollutants can damage and kill trees. Whether these mechanisms work exactly the same in nature, however, won't be known for certain until further scientific evidence comes in. Still, the disturbing laboratory tests suggesting how ozone in concentrations like those found in Los Angeles damages the needles of ponderosa and Jeffrey pines have to be taken seriously. So do experiments in which ozone has reduced white pines' annual growth by 70 percent and accelerated normal nutrient loss from leaves of silver fir, Norway spruce, and beech, or other experiments that show how acid rain can damage red spruce.

In the end, it may be impossible to trace today's temperate forest decline back to any single cause. Most likely, multiple stresses work together to do the job: forests bombarded by acid rain, ozone, and other air pollutants grow more susceptible to cold winters and other natural events. But even if it takes aggravated assault—a combination of natural and man-made forces—to finally kill off a tree or a forest, air pollution is still partly to blame.

Air pollution is also beginning to appear in and around the tropical forests of Africa, Asia, and Latin America, say scientists who attended an international conference in August 1990 on biomass (vegetation) burning. They report that both ozone and acid rain are becoming significant in the tropics. Evidence presented at the conference showed ozone levels over broad regions of West Africa now reaching levels comparable to those over the eastern United States. Jack Foshman, of NASA, reported similar findings for Indonesia and Brazil. Other scientists report acidity in rainfall in the Ivory Coast, the Congo, and the Amazon comparable to that believed to be damaging trees in the eastern United States. Fire from land clearing is a major cause of these pollution problems in the tropics, and it also contributes to the global greenhouse problem. Fire and deforestation already account for about 15 percent of the warming anticipated from the buildup of CO^2, ozone, and other greenhouse gases.

THE FORCES BEHIND TROPICAL FOREST LOSS

Thanks to news coverage, public television documentaries, the concern of such celebrities as Paul McCartney, Robert Redford, Tom Cruise, Rita Coolidge, Sting, R.E.M., Bette Midler, and the Grateful Dead, and the campaigns of environmental groups, the need to save tropical forests has reached at least the slogan-and-bumper-sticker stage in the United States. But, unless the underlying causes of forest destruction are faced squarely and addressed right now, the benefits we derive from tropical forests may be lost.

What are these key forces?

1. *Unequal distribution of resources.* Experts agree that not everyone benefits equally—or has the same chance to benefit—from the bounty of tropical forests. As Peter Raven, Director of the Missouri Botanical Garden, puts it, the quarter of the world's people who live in industrial nations control at least 80 percent of Earth's resources. Says Stanford University biologist

Paul Ehrlich, who has multiplied the number of people by some measure of their affluence and multiplied that number by the environmental effects of the technologies used to attain affluence, "an American baby is about 250 times the threat to world environment and resources as a Bangladeshi baby." Other experts think that the ratio is much lower, but, even if the multiplier is only 40 rather than 250, the message is clear: not all the world's citizens consume the same amount of the world's resources.

However, this is not simply a we-they, North-South issue. Differences in wealth exist *within* tropical cultures, too. The affluent in developing countries have consumerist, wasteful life styles similar to those of wealthy Americans. Their world is entirely different from the shantytowns of the urban and rural poor.

Land is the resource most unfairly distributed. In Latin America, just 7 percent of all landowners control 93 percent of the region's arable land. About 20 million Latin Americans have no land at all or have plots too small to grow enough to feed themselves and their families. In many agricultural nations, where the vast majority of people are poor and live far from any kind of market, owning enough land can mean the difference between starvation and survival.

2. *Rapid population growth.* The human population reached 5 billion in 1987—twice the 1950 population. Another billion will be with us by this century's end. "If historians in the distant future are able to look back at the twentieth century, they will undoubtedly write about population change as one of its most remarkable features," writes Robert Repetto of the World Resources Institute in *The Global Possible.* "Our generation is witnessing the flood crest of population growth. Already in this century, world population has increased threefold. From tens of thousands of years in neolithic times and hundreds of years at the start of the industrial age, the time required to double the population has shortened in this half of the twentieth century to just thirty-five years."

Although the *rate* of human population growth has slowed in recent years, our total numbers won't stop increasing anytime soon. Each year there are about 90 million more of us. In effect, we are adding to the world the equivalent of another Mexico each year. Global population is now expected to top 10 billion—and maybe even reach a hard-to-imagine 14 billion—by the time it finally stabilizes, probably late in the next century.

Some population watchers believe that there are already more of us than Earth can long support, at least in the manner that we've become accustomed to in developed nations. One is Paul Ehrlich. In 1989, he told the American Institute of Biological Sciences that "it is possible to support today's population of approximately 5.5 billion people only because humanity collectively is doing something that no prudent family would consider: squandering its inheritance. We are living on our capital—a one-time bonanza of fossil fuels, high-grade mineral ores, Pleistocene groundwater, topsoil, and biodiversity."

If Ehrlich is right, forests won't be able to withstand the onslaught for long. Population growth rates have dropped sharply in industrial nations after peaking in the postwar "baby boom," but in many tropical countries they are just beginning to decline. In some, primarily in Africa, population growth rates have not slowed at all; Zaire's annual growth rate is expected to continue rising until the turn of the century and its population to stabilize at 200 million by 2045—a dramatic increase over its 1987 level of 33 million!

Clearly, the pressure to cut trees for fuelwood or timber or to clear forests for mining or new farmland will intensify unless something gives. Population growth brings into question more than the number of people Earth can support. How fast can governments create educational opportunities, health care, housing, and social services to meet the needs of their teeming millions?

3. *Poverty*. Forty percent of the population of developing nations—about 1.2 billion people—live in absolute grinding poverty. Two-thirds of these people consume less than 90 percent of the calories needed to lead an active working life. Some 300 to 400 million people consume less than 80 percent of this critical minimum—too little to prevent stunted growth and serious health risks. More than 14 million children under four years of age starve to death each year in tropical and subtropical nations. At least a million older people do, too. Worldwide, starvation causes one out of every three deaths.

A key part of the solution is to promote economic development that doesn't deplete the natural resource base. In most tropical countries, the 1980s were a lost decade. Economies stagnated. Populations grew. Few new jobs were created. Millions of people were forced to forage for a living in urban slums and the countryside, including the tropical forest.

4. *Debt.* Encouraged by banks newly awash in oil money, developing nations borrowed heavily in the 1970s from industrial nations. They also took out big loans from such international institutions as the World Bank. But rising prices for petroleum products, increasing interest rates, and a global recession have caught these countries in a vise. Most can't pay back their loans. Stuck with interest payments on enormous debts, tropical nations can't get ahead, so they continue to regard their forests either as products for export—to bring in needed foreign dollars—or as less important than immediate needs such as farming, mining, or gathering fuelwood.

Together, the developing nations' debt now totals about $1 trillion. A 1 percent rise in U.S. interest rates could quickly add another $8 billion to this total. To make interest payments on their debts, developing nations desperately need cash, and the most ready source for many comes from cutting down forests, either to get hardwoods or to raise cattle or grow export crops. Brazil, for example, owed about $115 billion in foreign debts in 1989 and spent nearly 42 percent of its export earnings on debt payments. According to the World Bank, the net cash flow from poor countries to rich ones now approaches $50 billion a year. Former West German Chancellor Willy Brandt has likened the developing nations' debt payments to a "blood transfusion from the sick to the healthy." Indeed, if rich countries want tropical forests to survive, it's up to them to see that the transfusion flows in the other direction.

For simplicity's sake, these four driving forces of tropical deforestation are discussed separately here, but they obviously interact in various ways. In the Philippines, for example, inequitable resource distribution, explosive population growth, poverty, debt, and deforestation feed on each other. The population there has tripled since independence in 1946, but a few wealthy families and corporations own most of the land. Poor people are pushed onto steep, forested hillsides, which they clear to grow food. Twice-yearly monsoons rush down the denuded slopes, flooding lowlands and carrying off topsoil that silts up reservoirs behind hydroelectric plants and ruins estuaries and spawning grounds. The ruined fisheries mean more hunger among a people whose main protein source is fish, as well as less foreign exchange with which to service international debt. Variations on this vicious circle exist throughout the tropics.

Another phenomenon that may seem unrelated—the role of women in many tropical societies and cultures—also plays a part in forest loss. In central African villages, for example, women raise most of the food and gather the fuelwood and, while doing so, inadvertently do most of the damage to forests. Yet, ironically, women continue to be excluded from the discussion when, say, officials visit a village to introduce new farming techniques or to propose agroforestry or reforestation projects. Small wonder that most such projects fail. In ways too seldom noticed, the fate of a tropical nation's forests is tied to that of its women. Unless they have a say in planning and economic decisions—unless their lot improves enough to guarantee access to income, medical care, and family planning services—population growth and poverty will continue unabated, making forestry reform a lost cause.

Logging, cattle ranching, colonization, mining, and fuelwood gathering may be the visible causes of tropical forest loss, but they are mere symptoms of the underlying causes that drive the process. These convergent economic and social forces, in part driven by demand in industrial countries, will largely determine whether tropical forests, indigenous peoples, and still-unnamed species survive. Since the chain of events that leads to deforestation differs from one country to another, the way these forces interact as the future unfolds will bear the stamp of each forested region's unique history and environment. With that in mind, let's now turn from the wide-angle lens employed in this chapter to a close-up look at how the world's largest tropical rain forest is faring.

3

Amazônia: The Last Frontier?

If the Amazon forest disappears, it is likely
that all the other tropical forests of the
planet will have preceded it over the
horizon. If any tropical forest in the world
is redeemable, on the other hand, it is the
Amazonian forest—the world's largest and
least ravaged and most important.

ROGER D. STONE
Dreams of Amazônia

The Amazon is to rain forests as Antarctica is to ice. Both tropical
forests and ice can be found outside regional storehouses, but not
in such quantity or to such astonishing effect. Amazônia—South
America's heartland—covers 2.5 million square miles in parts
of Brazil, Bolivia, Colombia, Ecuador, French Guiana, Guyana,
Peru, Suriname, and Venezuela. It's "a piece of terrain so huge
it remains an abstraction to most people," writes Tad Szulc in
Bordering on Trouble: Resources and Politics in Latin America:
"Swooping low in a small plane over the rainforest is like flying
over an endless green ocean." If Amazônia were an independent
country, it would be the ninth largest nation on earth.

Snaking through the basin's center, the powerful Amazon River
"lends itself to the sort of statements that made Ripley famous,"
writes Catherine Caufield in *In the Rainforest*. "It has more than
a thousand tributaries, several of which are larger than the Mississippi." Caufield notes that oceangoing vessels can cruise all the
way to Iquitos, in Peru, 2,300 miles inland. One-fifth of Earth's
fresh water flows through the Amazon every day, more water than
the next eight biggest rivers together carry. "Marajó, an island in
the Amazon estuary, is the size of Switzerland. At the river's
mouth its north and south banks are farther apart than are Paris
and London."

Over three-fifths of the Amazon Basin lies in Brazil. Brazil's 828-million-acre endowment of forest is triple that of the next two leading rain forest nations, Indonesia and Zaire, combined. The sheer magnitude of this forest can make the Amazon seem indestructible—"a green monster so huge and vital that it could not possibly disappear," as Eugene Linden of *Time* magazine put it in 1989. But, like tropical forests throughout the world, the Amazon is only too destructible. Over the past two decades, enormous tracts of these forests—by some accounts the richest on Earth—have literally gone up in smoke.

Competition for the vast Amazonian forest is fierce. The poor and landless need access to land and a future. The Amerindians, the rubber tappers, and the people who make a living from the river want to stay where they are, masterfully plying their trades and traditions. Conservationists and environmentalists want to preserve the region's biodiversity and keep rainfall, climate, and vegetation patterns from changing abruptly. Governments of the region look to the forest to absorb the landless and to unleash the economic wealth of Amazônia's timber, minerals, soils, and energy. The nation's creditors also eye the same resources as a means to pay back near-crippling debt—$115 billion in Brazil's case.

Can all these claims be satisfied without bringing about environmental disaster? Theoretically, there's enough forest to go around, but conflicts over who gets what can't be resolved easily.

"OPENING UP"

To understand the causes of destruction in the Amazon, we need to look first to the region's political and economic history. In 1937, during the administration of President Vargas, Brazil's military formulated its own strategy for developing the region. As its ideologue, General Golbery, put it, Brazil needs to "inundate the Amazon forest with civilization." This has been the basic military doctrine and philosophy of action for half a century.

Philosophy became fact in 1966. During a boat trip on the Amazon aboard the *Rosa da Fonseca*, President Castelo Branco (in office from 1964 to 1967) announced his "Operation Amazonica" to a select group of businessmen. As Susanna Hecht and Alexander Cockburn tell the story in *The Fate of the Forest: Developers, Destroyers, and Defenders of the Amazon,* the president explained to his guests how "development poles" would be established in key areas. Tax breaks, land concessions, trade arrangements, sweetheart loans, and a variety of credits would be made available to entrepreneurs to develop industry, mining, commercial agriculture, and other enterprises in the Amazon. He also announced plans to encourage immigration and settlement, to develop roads, agriculture, and livestock, and to investigate the development potential of the region's minerals, fish, and timber. Soon entrepreneurs—over half from São Paulo's elite families—flooded into the region, eager to take advantage of the new "free trade" zone in Manaus. Thus began the Amazonian boom—the rush to develop cattle ranches and to colonize the "empty lands."

A few years later, Brazil's next president, Emilio Garrastazú Medici (1969–74), took another step to open up the Amazon. Medici "was so moved by representations made to him on a visit in the late 1960s to Brazil's dry, overpopulated, and poverty stricken Northeast region that he promised to resettle many of the poor in the 'land of milk and honey'—the Amazon Basin," writes Alan Grainger in *The Ecologist.* Making good on his word, he launched the "National Integration Plan" that established the National Colonization and Agrarian Reform Institute (INCRA) and sponsored an immigration program to bring new settlers into the Amazon. The plan also placed under federal government control all untitled lands located along the new highway system. INCRA was to administer some 540 million acres, or 850,000 square miles—a piece of real estate larger than all but 11 nations.

Within two years the colonization program was failing. Only 8,000 colonists came to occupy these new lands, and most of them were heading for other sites, new villages, or back to the shantytowns of the country's major cities. It turned out that no colonist could succeed on the average 240-acre plot without finding a second, off-site job. Yet, jobs near to the small farms were few, and access to adjacent forests was closing as cattle ranching and deforestation encroached. Violence brewed, and one in three small farmers left their plots after receiving threats to their lives from those amassing ever-larger land holdings.

The government's next response was to create the "Program for Amazonian Development." With colonization floundering, those in power turned to large, capital-intensive projects in mining, timber, and cattle. This shift of focus from small-scale farming to a corporate approach to development brought a new buzzword into financial circles: "export-led development." Governments would provide incentives to stimulate the production of commodities for sale abroad to earn foreign currencies to help pay the nation's debt and finance economic development.

In 1986 came the fourth recipe for developing Amazônia—this time, the *Calha Norte,* a strip of land 100 miles wide stretching along Brazil's border for 4,000 miles, from Guiana to Peru. Developed by the National Security Council, this plan would be the first under civilian supervision and would cover the tribal lands of 51 groups of indigenous peoples and areas inhabited by more than 20,000 gold miners and an untold number of land speculators.

Slated to cover the frontier zone, the rivers, and the hinterlands, this geographically wide ranging plan also had to involve some cooperation with neighboring Amazonian countries. Indeed, there are provisions for cross-border road building, drug-traffic control, increased military installations and facilities along the borders, and border marking. While left rather vague, the *Calha Norte* plan also called for a new policy toward Amerindians in the area, and new highways, hydropower facilities, and social services.

Ironically, the very people who had evolved ways to live and work in the Amazon—the Amerindians, the river-based settlers, and the rubber tappers—were not included in these grand plans. Their lands were being overrun, their youth lured to the gold fields by the promise of quick wealth, and their cultures decimated. A particularly grievous assault was the *perimenal norte* highway, which sliced through Yanomami tribal lands.

Three years into Brazil's first civilian administration in almost two decades came government's most recent plan for the Amazon region. In 1988, under mounting international pressure to control tropical deforestation and to respect Amerindian and rubber-tapper lands, President José Sarney initiated a relatively open process to formulate his new policy on the environment. Released in 1988, *Nossa Natureza* ("Our Nature") revealed Brazil's environmental perspective on Amazonian development and explicitly recognized forest peoples. The plan specified action on such major problems as pollution from gold mining and promised to protect the environment of the tribal peoples, those who depended on the river for their way of life, and other forest dwellers. Sarney's plan also called for the establishment of reserves for forest groups, the suspension of inappropriate subsidies for cattle ranching and other enterprises, the creation of new national parks and national forests, and agro-ecological zoning. Conspicuously absent from the plan was reference to further colonization, road construction, and dam building.

Critics of *Nossa Natureza* observe that many features of the 1960s development policies in the Amazon continue business-as-usual in 1990: new roads are being built, main access roads are being paved, and work on dams is continuing. Yet, the significant drop in deforestation rates reported for 1988 and 1989, following the extreme 1987 figures, suggests that elements of the new policy are working. Perhaps most significant among these has been the elimination of incentives to cattle ranching.

PRESSURES ON AMAZÔNIA'S PEOPLE

Throughout history, pioneers have migrated to the wilderness, searching for land and a better life. Often, these settlers face disappointment when they reach "the promised land." No earthly paradise awaits the weary; only what William Bradford called, as he stepped off the *Mayflower*, a "hideous and desolate wilderness." To transform these wilds into the paradise of their dreams, pioneers on every continent have hacked open vast tracts of forest, making way for homes, roads, crops, livestock, and, ultimately, cities and towns, often displacing indigenous populations in the process.

Brazil's forestlands have been no exception. There, forest is cleared by the new colonists escaping drought in Brazil's arid Northeast, the slums of São Paulo or Rio, or joblessness stemming from mechanization of agriculture in the South. Others are simply moving on after their soils are exhausted or they are run off their land by the work crews building roads and dams or by the gangs defending lands newly cleared for ranching. The thousands of small-scale gold prospectors and miners only make the situation worse by disrupting streams, soils, and rural societies. The upshot is constant uncertainty and insecurity for the old and new residents alike. With no bankable future themselves, migrants have little incentive to care for the land and the forest, and even the long-term residents of the forest—the Amerindians, riverine peoples, and rubber tappers who have fished, hunted, grown crops, and gathered other forest products for decades or centuries—face violent conflicts over land and loss of basic resources, not to mention the ravages caused by disease and social breakdown.

Longtime residents of the region have been violated before, starting five centuries ago when the Spanish, Portuguese, and other European colonizers arrived in Amazônia. From the 1800s through World War II, thousands of rubber tappers roamed the wilderness to gather the valuable latex. Mechanized ways to move latex to markets fast enough to meet rising demand were introduced during the 1930s and 1940s. Motorboats plied the rivers, and a new inland railroad was built. During the same period, international conflict heated up over the political status of what is now the Brazilian state Acre, but was once part of Bolivian territory.

Powerful individuals have also tried to transform Amazônia—local residents, local culture, and the forest be damned. As early as 1928, Henry Ford tried to make his mark there with an enormous rubber plantation that gradually collapsed, thanks to an excess of fungus and a shortage of labor. Four decades later, with many colossal failed experiments on record in the interim, the American billionaire Daniel K. Ludwig tried again. Ludwig began building a 3-million-acre agro-industrial complex along the Jari River in 1967. By clearing natural forest to create vast plantations of exotic trees, Ludwig hoped to supply a pulp mill. On other lands, he tried to get rice and livestock started. Whole new villages were carved out of wild jungle. However, the soils lost their

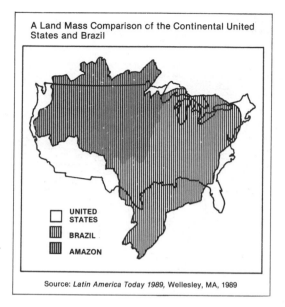

A Land Mass Comparison of the Continental United States and Brazil

UNITED STATES
BRAZIL
AMAZON

Source: *Latin America Today 1989*, Wellesley, MA, 1989

productivity, and enormous cost overruns finally exhausted even the multimillionaire.

Apart from the pain inflicted upon them by foreign invaders and opportunists, the forest, traditional forest peoples, and new colonists have also been the victims of Brazil's cultural pride. As Tad Szulc wrote in *Bordering on Trouble*, "the Brazilian move north [into Amazônia] resembles the winning of the American West more than a century ago; and, interestingly, the Brazilians . . . in the North are pleased and fascinated by the comparison, which they had noted themselves." Much as the American West figured in the hopes and dreams of all Americans until the frontier closed, in Brazil the Amazon is considered the playing field of economic destiny. (Small wonder that Brazilian leaders resent hypocritical attacks on their development plans by countries, like the United States, that converted large tracts of forests as they urbanized and industrialized and are now demanding interest payments on Brazil's debt.)

SAVE THE BRAZILIAN RAIN FORESTS

MEANWHILE, BACK IN THE PACIFIC NORTHWEST....

LAND HUNGER

In this context of mixed motives and pressing needs, it's not
surprising that land ownership is the major bone of contention
between forest dwellers and the Brazilian government. What is
surprising is how concentrated landholdings are in Brazil. In 1985,
fully 61 percent of the land in the Amazonian state of Rondônia
was held by a mere 2 percent of the landowners, while 53 percent
of the landowners collectively held title to only 13 percent! Such
skewed ownership patterns hurt the poor: the large tracts of land
held by wealthy individuals or corporations have historically been
off limits to forest dwellers, most of whom can't find enough land
to survive.

Like people who have tried to colonize other tropical rain forest
areas, many of these pioneers have found that their dream of a
new life in the jungle has become a nightmare in a "green hell."

Once in the Amazon, writes Grainger, many settlers move on because they "didn't like what they found: heavy rain, insects, but worst of all, the fertility of the land was spent after it had delivered three crops." Few migrants are prepared for what they find in the wet and humid Amazon because most come either from the arid Northeast or, more recently, from the fertile lands and temperate climate of Southern Brazil.

Some pioneers have been lucky: their land has proved more fertile than most, or they have learned from experienced neighbors how to grow crops successfully. But even the fortunate few still face violent battles for land ownership. "Explosive and uncontrolled migration, instead of easing social conflicts, has simply moved them into the rain forest," reports Philip Bennett of the *Boston Globe*. As a result, "in the land without men, there is now a shortage of land. Deforestation and gunfire determine who controls it."

Hecht and Cockburn report that "between 1972 and 1976 land prices in the State of Acre increased by between 1,000 and 2,000 percent, and more than a third of the State, nearly 12 million acres, changed hands." During the 1970s and 1980s, people with little or no land could find short-term work clearing forests at the frontier. Once the land was cleared, however, employment ceased and the incentive to cave in to speculators grew. A so-called small holder with legal title could sell his cleared plot after one year for up to five years' worth of wages.

For buyers, land became an important hedge against inflation. Other factors also stimulated land grabbing in the region. Mineral surveys began showing that reserves of iron, gold, diamonds, and other ores are far more extensive and valuable than expected. Timber for building was growing scarce in the country as the southern *Araucaria* forests were depleted, and the urban poor were demanding ever more charcoal, which is made from wood. With the expanding system of roads, especially around the development poles, once-inaccessible lands commanded four to ten times the price of plots further inland, while cleared lands brought 30 percent higher prices than those still forested since clearing was one of the legal requirements of establishing ownership.

DAMS, ROADS, AND MEGADEVELOPMENT PROJECTS

From 1981 to 1983, the World Bank earmarked approximately $450 million to Brazil for the *Polonoroeste* ("Northwest Development Pole") land settlement and development project in Rondônia and Matto Grosso. Most of the funds were to go for the paving of a road, innocuously called BR-364, and the construction of feeder roads. These byways cut through the heart of the region's previously intact forests and attracted over 200,000 landless migrants in 1989 alone. It may, as the government claimed, be "the biggest land reform ever tried," but the *Polonoroeste* project has earned another distinction too: Brazil's highest deforestation rates.

In 1987, the World Bank's president, Barber Conable, called *Polonoroeste* a "sobering example of an environmentally sound effort that went wrong." "The Bank" he went on, "misread the human, institutional, and physical realities of the jungle and the frontier. . . . Protective measures to shelter fragile land and tribal peoples were included; they were not, however, carefully timed, or adequately monitored." Indeed. According to the terms of the loans, 17 tribal areas and 4 nature reserves were to receive appropriate legal status. By early 1990, 10 tribal areas and the 4 nature reserves were still awaiting legal protection.

Despite an international outcry over the *Polonoroeste* project, in early 1990 the World Bank was negotiating another *Polonoroeste* loan. Some remain critical of the Bank's role in Amazônia, though the new project does contain many "green" elements, including an "agro-ecological zoning" system for tying land use to sound ecology. If the Bank and the government make good on their promises, and if settlers in the Amazon region respect the zoning scheme, only about 20 percent of the project territory will be used for agriculture, and much of this land is already populated, deforested, and known to be nutrient-rich enough to support crops. Roughly 10 million acres will be designated as "extractive reserves"—government lands available for long-term use by people who reap rubber, Brazil nuts, fruit, and other nontimber products. Another 500,000 acres will be used for forest-management experiments. Five million acres are to be set aside for nature reserves, and more than 12 million for tribal peoples' exclusive use.

The construction of huge hydroelectric dams has also marked the Amazon indelibly, and the search for energy is just beginning. Only three dams had been completed in Amazônia by late 1989, but they have transformed huge tracts of land. The Balbina Dam on the Uatumá River was built to provide half of Manaus' electricity. Its reservoir covered 900 square miles—an area almost half the size of Delaware. The Tucuruí Dam in Pará also flooded vast stretches of forest and forced thousands of families to evacuate. Reportedly, six towns were completely inundated, and several Indian reserves were at least partially flooded. The huge, stagnant timber-lined lakes created by these dams are made-to-order breeding grounds for malaria-carrying mosquitoes and for snails that transmit schistosomiasis, a debilitating and often fatal parasitic disease.

If the trees and other plants aren't removed from tropical rain forests before they are flooded, the vegetation can rot very quickly, jeopardizing the dam itself and creating an ugly, stinking mess. The Brokopondo Dam on the Suriname River, for example, flooded 570 square miles of rain forest. "As the trees and underbrush decomposed, they produced enough hydrogen sulfide gas to raise a howl of complaint many miles downstream," write Marc Reisner and Ronald H. McDonald in *Bordering on Trouble: Resources and Politics in Latin America*. "For two years, workers at the dam wore gas masks. The decomposing vegetation made the water so harshly acidic that it corroded the dam's cooling system, which cost $4 million to repair. . . . The oxygen-deficient water stunned and killed fish for fifty miles downriver." Some experts say that rapid decomposition is beginning to plague Brazil's Tucuruí too.

Like roads, dams are also magnets for economic development, much of it environmentally unsound. The few thousand square miles flooded by dams so far may seem a pittance compared to the amount of forest that cattle ranchers and farmers have burned, but the availability of more electricity typically lures mining companies and other industries to the region. Already, several ambitious industrial projects are cranking up around dams. By far the largest, the Grande Carajás, was established a decade ago to exploit the region's huge deposits of iron ore, copper, manganese, nickel, bauxite, and gold. At an estimated cost of $3.5 billion, the scheme encompasses 324,000 square miles in the eastern Amazon—an area larger than Texas and equal to more than 10 percent of Brazil's total land area.

Just one part of this mammoth project is operating at full tilt today: an iron ore mine that started up in 1985. The mine itself has not harmed the surrounding forests appreciably, but the smelters that convert iron ore into pig iron are powered by charcoal made from rain forest trees. Four smelters are currently operating in Marabá, and nearly 25 more are planned. According to Dennis J. Mahar of the World Bank, which lent $304 million to finance the iron ore mine and the railway that transports ore and pig iron to the coast, more than a million tons of charcoal a year will eventually be needed to feed the smelters. Eucalyptus plantations have been started to supply some of this wood, but Mahar estimates that between 1,350,000 and 3 million acres of land will be deforested to feed the smelters. Is this scheme just robbing Peter to pay Paul? A team of West German consultants concluded that creating fuelwood plantations, the only realistic alternative to cutting the forests, is not economically viable here, and Brazil's former secretary of the environment, Paulo Nogueira Neto, said publicly that the whole eastern Amazon region could face extermination if the pig-iron and steel industries continue to grow.

The Grande Carajás has brought other woes to eastern Amazônia, too. Thousands of Brazilians have migrated into this area, hoping for jobs at gold mines, dams, railroads, and the like. Between 1980 and 1985, Marabá's population more than doubled—from 60,000 to 130,000. This boom has only intensified deforestation and violent clashes over land that began in the 1960s when the Belém-Brasília highway was completed.

Worries about *Polonoreste* and other boom towns and boom regions gone awry are grounded in some staggering statistics. According to Tad Szulc, between 1970 and 1980, the population of one town in the state of Pará, Conceição do Araguaia, increased from 27,000 to 112,000. Meanwhile, Tucuruí increased from 10,000 people to 61,000, and the population of Porto Velho, Rondônia's capital, grew from 65,000 to 202,000. What these numbers demonstrate, writes Szulc, is the extent to which "millions of desperate Brazilians are determined to colonize the Amazon Basin, which looms as a modern El Dorado to those who want to get rich quick and as a last hope to those who simply want to improve their lots and leave their children some kind of future."

HOOVES

By the mid-1960s, Brazil's military government realized that domestic demand for beef was growing rapidly. It had also decided that rising international demand provided a good opportunity to earn much-needed foreign exchange. The best place to support livestock enterprises, it figured, was Amazônia.

This decision has changed the face of Amazônia. Some 600 cattle ranches averaging 50,000 acres each have been established in the region with the help of subsidized long-term loans, tax credits that cover most of the investment costs, tax holidays, and write-offs. According to economist Robert Repetto of the World Resources Institute, large ranches totalling some 30 million acres have produced only about 9 percent of the meat that they were supposed to deliver, which translates into $2.5 billion that the government will never see for its efforts. Cattle ranches on once-forested lands failed partly because of weeds. Keeping pastures free of brush and other unwanted plants proved to be a losing battle. Today, roughly 30 percent of the large ranches have been abandoned, and 40 percent have produced no net returns. According to one survey, only three of these projects turned a serious profit, and many analysts now believe that livestock production in Amazônia is simply not profitable without subsidies or gains made through land speculation. In other words, cattle ranching is not so much a way to put meat on the table or money in the public coffers as it is a way for wealthy Brazilians to beat inflation.

Such ghost ranching takes a toll. Brazil's tax revenues aren't what they should be, and the money spent on subsidies could have been invested much more profitably. Species losses, soil degradation, climate changes, and muddied streams will reduce future options for everyone. And, of course, the traditional residents of the forest are losing their homes and livelihoods.

This indictment notwithstanding, tropical forests can accommodate small-scale ranching just as they can withstand shifting cultivation under some circumstances. Indeed, the uncertainties of agricultural production in the interior of the Amazon, the distance to markets, and the need to relocate periodically all make cattle ranching appealing, and in small-scale enterprises, farmers *cum* ranchers can produce both milk and meat. Cattle raising requires comparatively little time, so the small-time farmer-rancher is free to work for wages or tend other crops. And when the plot's soils wear out, the pasture will give the farm family a few more years on the site. To top it off, pasturelands fetch greater prices than depleted croplands and strengthen the farmer-rancher's claim to the parcel.

Eventually, brush has its way, however, and few pastures last for more than a decade. More than half of the lands already cleared for pasture have been abandoned, and many scientists believe that it will take about a century for abandoned pasturelands to revert to something resembling a forest—and that's only if they have not been severely burned. Where fire has been used intensively, as demonstrated in a test plot in Venezuela, it may take up to 80 years just to reestablish half of the original vegetation. Whatever benefits ranchers or farmers derive from livestock thus come at a high public cost.

Unlike other tropical areas, such as Central America, where beef exports are high, Amazônia is a net beef importer. Even if beef were more plentiful, it couldn't be exported overseas from the region because of the presence of hoof-and-mouth disease. The wealth generated by cattle ranching is definitely not being spread around, much less used to help the poor in Amazônia.

GOLD FEVER

Since about 1980, a modern-day gold rush has been taking place in Amazônia. Most of the prospectors are small-time and so-called placer mine operators (*garimpeiros*) who work the stream beds and river banks searching for nuggets, dust, and veins of gold.

Since most operate outside the government controls that regulate mining, they are considered illegal. Their ranks have already swollen to between 1 and 1.5 million, and, according to the scarce information available, most are young men between the ages of 15 and 25. Half are the sons of small farmers. Others drift into mining from unstable seasonal jobs. All are seeking social mobility and the chance to buy some land. As Hecht and Cockburn note, "for a small farmer ever under attack from internal and external difficulties and from the erratic nature of labor markets everywhere in the Amazon, the *garimpo* is a godsend." To the impact of the miners must be added that of the 2 to 3 million people who provide them with fuel, food, labor, transportation, and prostitutes.

According to Marc Dourojeanni of the Inter-American Development Bank and Maria Tereza Jorge Padua of the Brazilian conservation group FUNATURA, most of this clandestine gold passes out of Brazil down the rivers to Uruguay and then overseas. As Dourojeanni and Jorge Padua note in their forthcoming study on gold mining in the Amazon, the current boom that has sent prospectors and miners into the farthest reaches of the Amazon, including Amerindian lands and national parks, has many causes. The price of gold is up. Road and air access to hinterlands has improved. Thanks to high unemployment throughout Brazil, the labor supply is almost limitless. New small-scale technologies, such as mini-pumps, boats, and dredging equipment, are now available, and, not least, government policy allows such mining.

Amazônia's gold is impressive. The official production figure for Brazil in 1980 was 13.8 tons, but many believe that 34.5 tons is closer to the mark. Of this amount, 88 percent was produced by *garimpeiros*. By 1989, the total production probably reached 295 tons, compared to a world total of 1,880 tons. Of this potential income, valued at $3.3 billion per year, the Brazilian government sees only about 15 percent. The rest leaves the country as contraband.

The techniques used to mine gold are particularly devastating to the forest. Small operators work with modest rafts, scuba gear, and pumps to separate ore from gravel. But large outfits barge dredges and bulldozers upstream, open up vast tracts of forest with this equipment, churn the soils, and separate ore from gravel with large-scale hydraulic pumps. In this process, streambeds are transformed, riverbanks are stripped bare of trees, drainage is altered, and the soils are turned upside down. According to Dourojeanni and Jorge Padua, whole upstream catchments are strewn with craters, as though they had been bombed.

Mercury—which can cause birth defects, brain damage, loss of muscle control, and death—is used in gold mining to help separate the gold ore from the gravel and sand. When the mercury is then burned off, mercury vapor escapes into the air and mercury ash forms. The vapor is inhaled or returned to earth in rain, and most of the ash is dumped into rivers, where it disrupts the food chain and contaminates the river fish that are a staple in the region. For each kilo of gold, about 1.32 kilos of mercury makes its way into the atmosphere or the river. Oil, garbage, and organic matter from gold camps also damage the environment, as do excessive hunting, logging, and fishing by the miners.

FIRES

As if these other insults to the rain forest weren't enough, fire itself has become a major force of degradation. As long as people have inhabited the Amazon, fires have been part of the region's cycle of destruction and renewal. But, in recent years, the number and scale of man-made fires has risen. "In the fall of 1976," writes Alex Shoumatoff in *Vanity Fair,* a "fire as big as Rhode Island was raging out of control on the Volkswagen AD ranch in Pará State, in eastern Amazônia," and on another ranch there, he writes, "the heat from the tremendous walls of flame was so intense that it created local fire storms, complete with thunder, lightning, and mini-tornadoes . . . huge trees that had been blasted into the air . . . had landed upside down with their root buttresses sticking up like the fins of crashed rocket ships."

Throughout the 1980s, fires ripped through vast swaths of Amazônia. "In 1987 there was so much fire that for weeks all of South America was covered by a dense veil of smoke," writes José Lutzenberger (now Brazil's environment minister) in *Earth Island Journal.* "In southern Brazil the sky appeared grey with smoke, the sun was weak and dark red and disappeared long before it touched the horizon in the evening.'' The aftermath of such fire storms can be surreal, too. As Hecht and Cockburn write in *The Fate of the Forest*, ''a soft ash mingles with the dust from the unpaved roads giving the people on whom the powder settles a spectral aspect, and the landscape itself the patina of death.''

In 1978, about 58,600 square miles, or some 3 percent of Brazil's Amazonian forest, had been cleared. By 1989, 153,000 square miles had been cleared, or roughly 8 percent of the original cover. In a mid-1990 communication to the World Resources Institute, Alberto Setzer of Brazil's Space Research Institute noted that, based upon his recent satellite analysis, the average annual deforestation rate during the 1980s had been 8,160 square miles, or 5.2 million acres per year. Obviously, actual losses vary from one year to another. In 1987, the peak year of fire and clearing, some 20 million acres were lost.

THE ENVIRONMENTAL PRICE

The year 1987 was an exceptionally bad one for Brazil's Amazonian forest. It was the last year that tax credits were available to landholders who cleared their Amazonian holdings, and many large landowners no doubt pulled out all the stops while they could. By 1988 and 1989, clearing had decreased by at least 40 percent, thanks to government intervention and wetter weather. But even so, *de*forestation rates far exceed *re*forestation rates, and estimates for deforestation in 1988 and 1989 were three times greater than those for the early 1980s.

Much more difficult to document is the impact of deforestation on the region's species. No one is taking a head count, though experts are hazarding ballpark estimates. Writing in *Scientific American,* Paul A. Colinvaux surmised that the region's rain forest ''is home to perhaps 80,000 plant species (including 600 kinds of palm alone) and possibly 30 million animal species, most of them insects.'' In a single 2.5-acre plot near Manaus on the Amazon River, researchers have identified 235 tree species larger than 2 inches in diameter. At least 2,000 fish species live in the waters of the Amazon River system, eight times the number found in the

Mississippi River and its tributaries and ten times the number found in all of Europe.

Their sheer numbers aside, Amazonian species include some of the largest and most interesting on Earth. One towering strain of bamboo can grow to more than 50 feet in height. One Amazonian lilac can reach the size of an average apple tree. Bright blue Morpho butterflies have 7-inch wingspans. One Amazon riverfish, the *piraraucú,* can grow to 7 feet and can weigh up to 170 pounds. A giant catfish, the *piraíba,* can weigh in at 300 pounds. The *matrinxâo,* another fish, is a wonder of productivity: it gains a pound for every two it eats. In a weight class of its own is the Amazonian manatee, a comically beefy, all-too-edible, and now endangered herbivore that can tip the scales at several tons.

As for which of these well-studied species' unknown kin and companions have survived radical changes in Amazônia's ecosystems, the best that scientists can do is to calculate *theoretically* the loss of species in relation to the loss of wild habitat, and this formula works for land-based creatures only. If about one-quarter of the world's conservatively estimated 10 million species live in the Amazon, as many experts believe, and if on average some 20 million acres of forest are cleared each year, around 10,000 species are facing severe threat and possible extinction each year. That's 30 species per day right now.

Deforestation at this scale and pace will alter Amazônia's climate, too. In the central Amazon, about three-fourths of all rainfall either evaporates directly into the atmosphere from leaves and soil or gets taken up by roots and transpired by plants back into the air. Only about one-fourth ever flows away in local streams and rivers. Yet, in deforested systems, the reverse is true: only one-fourth is returned to the atmosphere, and three-fourths flows out through waterways. In other words, deforestation keeps half of the rainfall from returning to the sky.

Perhaps the greatest impact of all upon the forest, and its myriad small stream and river ecosystems, will come from gold mining. Just one measure of the destruction taking place is the amount of soil turned over, piled, and moved again, typically into the waterways. Besides clogging streams, this practice uproots plants, leaving soils vulnerable to erosion. Dourojeanni and Jorge Padua estimate that some 1.75 billion cubic feet of soil is being displaced in this way each year. To this sum, they suggest adding the unmeasured amounts of forest soil upturned or moved in diamond or tin mining, land cleared for agriculture, and overgrazing. Equally unsettling, during the mining operation, entire stream banks are turned upside down, with some excavations running 15 feet deep. Some sites of 80,000 acres in small upstream tributaries have been ravaged so severely that the forest will recover only slowly.

As for mercury poisoning from mining, the toll is still unknown. Writing in *Ambio,* the journal of the Swedish Academy of Sciences, Olaf Malm reports that "there is good reason to suppose that serious injuries to the health of miners and local people have already taken place and that an enormous mercury contamination of the Amazon ecosystem is in progress." To find out, scientists from the University of London planned to launch a study in late 1990. Meanwhile, scattered evidence is appearing. According to the *New York Times,* 70 cases of mercury poisoning had been reported by mid-1990 in one town 150 miles downstream from the mining center of Tapajós, and nearly half the fish caught downstream from gold-mining operations in Pará, Rondônia, and Amapá were severely contaminated.

THE VANQUISHED

The people of Amazônia, newcomers and longtime inhabitants alike, are paying a high price for a shot at economic development or, more accurately, for unsound development. The luckiest pioneer settlers find jobs on larger farms and ranches or in the new cities, and a comparative few even manage to make a go of farming their own plots. Most of the rest become both victim and cause of land clearing, forfeiting any sense of place or security as they part with dreams of settling down. The very poorest have joined the destitute throngs already invading the gold fields, boom towns, or returning to the shantytowns (*favelas*) of São Paulo, Rio de Janeiro, and Brazil's other overcrowded and increasingly unstructured cities.

Of special concern among the hundreds of thousands who live in the forest and the millions of poor Brazilians throughout the country for whom Amazônia is a source of potential national wealth and real national pride are the Amerindians—long-time forest dwellers who face cultural extinction after thousands of years of living in the forest without destroying it.

Nearly 200 Amerindian tribes, each with its own language, customs, and history, have inhabited Amazônia's forests. From the time of the Spanish and Portuguese exploration of the Amazon, indigenous communities have been decimated by colonists and have fallen prey to such infectious diseases as influenza, whooping cough, and measles, which are deadly to long-isolated peoples who have no chance of building up resistance to them. This loss of life and land has continued in recent years, as farmers, ranchers, miners, engineers, and businessmen, not to mention researchers and reporters, have poured into the Amazon Basin. While at least 6 million native people lived in Brazilian Amazônia when Europeans first arrived around 1500, at most 250,000 survive today. According to Cultural Survival, an organization that tries to protect indigenous peoples' rights worldwide, one indigenous Brazilian society has died out every year since 1900.

Native communities succumb both directly and indirectly when colonists arrive. First, deforestation takes a tremendous direct toll, even on designated reserves. Where hydroelectric dams are erected, reservoirs can flood thousands of acres of tribal lands. Where colonists accompany the construction project and, as often happens, settle near the reservoir, indigenous peoples' water supplies and plant and animal resources can be jeopardized by deforestation, too. As native contact with colonists grows, so does the fatal incidence of malaria, measles, yellow fever, and now even AIDS. Even if native communities escape with their lives and manage to hold onto their lands, their cultures may still be at risk of extinction.

One of the larger indigenous Amazonian groups, living until recently more or less as they had for generations, is the Yanomami. More than 20,000 strong, these people occupy parts of northern Brazil and southern Venezuela and make their living hunting, gathering, and farming in ways that do not hurt the forest. Kenneth I. Taylor, former director of Survival International, spent two years living among the Yanomami and found no evidence "that they ever overused their resources or in any way degraded their environment." Like other Amazonian Indian tribes, he writes in *People of the Tropical Rainforest,* the Yanomami "live in the forest and are part of the forest. If they destroy it, they destroy themselves."

But how long can the Yanomami hold out against the invaders? In Brazil, where 9,000 Yanomami live, outside forces have in recent years begun to destroy this group's forests and way of life. According to *Earth Island Journal,* some 20,000 gold miners invaded Yanomami lands in northern Brazil in just four months in 1988, and 45,000 to 100,000 live there now. "The wildlife the Yanomami depend on has been driven away. . . . The rivers have been polluted. Native cultivation has been raided by hungry miners and . . . some native peoples have been killed in attempts to defend their food." Both native community members and miners have died in these violent clashes. Influenza and new strains of malaria had by mid-1989 claimed more than 50 native lives. In four villages, the annual death rate since 1987 has been 14 percent, infant mortality near the five large mines stands at 28 percent, and several indigenous groups have been reduced by half. Malnutrition is rampant. According to newspaper accounts in early 1990, the disappearance of game and fish has driven some members of this once-proud community to beg from the same miners who brought disease and pollution to the area.

The Yanomami's struggle has attracted considerable attention outside Brazil. For many years, Yanomami leader Davi Kopenawa has been fighting to protect his people's Amazonian homeland from further invasions, and in 1989 the United Nations Environment Programme gave him one of its annual Global 500 prizes. When he accepted the award, Kopenawa said: "I am not against the gold-panners. I am against the gold-panning because it leaves holes, it ruins the rivers and streams. The Yanomami do not do this, cut up the land, cut down trees, burn the forest. We are not enemies of nature. We are friends of nature because we live there in the woods."

In December 1989, the Brazilian government of then-President José Sarney ordered the miners out after federal courts declared the opening of Yanomami land illegal. But, after the miners staged protests and threatened guerrilla warfare, the government did an about-face. Miners were allowed to stay, confirming that Yanomami lands would be reduced from 3,600 to 800 square miles in a crazy-quilt pattern of 19 unconnected tracts surrounded by a "national park" open to mining. The Yanomami were not party to this negotiated settlement, under which the miners made only two concessions: not to carry weapons and to control mercury pollution.

In May 1990, it looked like the tide was turning for the Yanomami. Just two weeks after his inauguration in March 1990, Brazil's new President, Fernando Collor de Mello, flew to Roraima State and, in a widely publicized move, ordered the dynamiting of the miners' landing strips. The situation grew volatile as miners threatened to resort to helicopters, which do not need airstrips to land. As of mid-1990, the federal police had stopped blowing up airstrips. The *garimpeiros* have returned, and both environmental organizations and the Yanomami are again sending their urgent pleas to halt the invasions. No easy resolution to the conflict between the *garimpeiros* and the Yanomami is in sight.

MARTYR OF THE AMAZON

In December 1988, an act of violence in the isolated state of Acre catapulted Brazil's rain forest crisis into headlines around the world. A few days before Christmas, Francisco "Chico" Mendes, the leader of a local rural workers' union, was murdered at his home in the town of Xapurí. The son of a rubber tapper and a lifelong resident of the Amazon, Mendes had been leading a successful fight to save parts of the forest for rubber tappers and other forest-dwellers. Mendes' enemies apparently thought he had been too successful. In December 1990, a wealthy cattle rancher and his son were convicted of murder and sentenced to 19 years in prison.

Rubber tappers, called *seringueiros* in Brazil, pride themselves on wresting a living from the forest without damaging the trees. They collect latex from the trunks of wild rubber trees by making clean, sharp cuts through the layers of bark. "A man who makes poor cuts gets a terrible name," rubber tapper Valerio da Silva told the *New York Times*. "To damage a tree is as bad as killing a pregnant animal or not paying your debts." Rubber tappers also collect other forest products, including Brazil nuts, and they tend small home gardens.

Since rubber tappers can't make a living unless the forest is healthy and whole, they try to keep it that way. But, as cattle ranchers and land speculators flood into the region, rubber tappers, who generally hold no legal title to the forests, are pushed off the land as forests are cleared and burned. Since land speculators first arrived in the 1970s, tens of thousands of rubber tapper families have been driven from their forest homelands.

Since the late 1970s, however, Acre's rubber tappers have been fighting back. Spurred on by Mendes and other leaders, the forest dwellers have organized peaceful marches and human barricades to block the chain saws. Some of their victories are small, for example, getting an individual landowner to give up a particular claim. The biggest wins that the rubber tappers have scored so far include getting the government to set up publicly held "extractive reserves."

Chico Mendes' influence had spread far beyond Brazil's borders during his lifetime. In 1987, he was awarded one of the UN Environment Programme's Global 500 prizes; the following year, he received an award from The Better World Society for his work. At a 1987 meeting of the Inter-American Development Bank (IDB) in Miami, Mendes told finance ministers from around the world how a new IDB-funded paved road (an extension of BR-364 under construction in Acre) could devastate the area. Later in Washington, D.C., he pleaded his case with senators, representatives, and their staffs. Under pressure from Congress, IDB suspended its loan and began negotiating with the Brazilian government for more environmental safeguards.

The story didn't end there, though. Later, financing for this road (and another suspended earlier when rubber tappers and environmentalists complained) was reinstated after the Brazilian government agreed to establish more extractive reserves, a new national forest, and a program to enforce regulations against illegal forest burning. In this deal making, a precedent was set at the IDB: before reinstating its loan, IDB representatives discussed the road with Acre's Indians and rubber tappers and secured their support for the project. Says Barbara Bramble of the National Wildlife Federation: "The IDB certainly deserves some credit." But, she adds, "we'll have to see if the banks will do this without someone being murdered, thousands of protest letters, and hundreds of front-page stories."

Meanwhile, bloody battles over land rage on in Acre and throughout the western Amazon. According to Amnesty International, hundreds of people have been killed in regional land disputes, including native Amazonians, small farmers, trade unionists, and lawyers and priests who work with small farmer organizations. Several death threats had been directed at Mendes in the months before his murder, and police had assigned him bodyguards. His successor, Osmarino Amancio Rodrigues, became the target of such threats as soon as he stepped into Mendes' shoes. And not only celebrated figures are at risk: nearly one thousand rubber tappers, Indians, and union activists have been killed over the past decade in land disputes.

Mendes' murder sparked an international outcry. The U.S. Senate condemned the act and demanded that the killers be found and punished. Mendes became a folk hero overnight. His life is being chronicled in at least five books and in several feature films and documentaries, including one by the producers of *Batman* and *Rain Man*. A float honoring Mendes was part of the 1990 Carnival celebration in Rio de Janeiro. Starting in 1990, several European nations, led by Spain, plan to make December 22—the date of Mendes' death—a day to remember the Amazonian rain forest. Inevitably, though, the publicity will fade, and when it does, Mendes' companions in the fight to save Brazil's rain forests hope that his message will live on. As Mendes told reporter Philip Bennett a few months before his death, "what we demand is a complete reorientation of Brazil's approach to the Amazon. It is the last hope for the rain forest, which is the last hope for man."

NEW LIFE FROM RAVAGED GROUND

In *Amazônia, Que Hacer?* (*What to Do?*), Marc Dourojeanni outlines a daring plan for Amazônia, one in which a self-sustaining landscape maintains natural cycles and biological diversity and one that offers social and economic opportunities and a decent standard of living for local residents. In this plan, the long-term needs of the local people come before exports and most of the region is kept in forest cover, but a steady harvest of forest products and nature conservation are also part of the scheme.

In this mixed landscape, some parcels would be tilled intensively to raise annual crops, while larger portions still would be planted in permanent crops. Still others would contain cattle that feed on residues from forestry and agriculture. Where the soils are poor, livestock and agriculture would be rotated with forest crops. Timber, fruit, nuts, chemicals, and game would be carefully extracted from less than half of the land. Some streams and lakes would be managed to produce fish and wildlife, and mining, oil extraction, and energy production would take place under strict environmental safeguards.

People are a big part of the ecosystem that Dourojeanni has in mind. In areas near borders, protected areas would help governments to secure their boundaries, back away from confrontation, and quell the mania to settle frontier areas. Nature-oriented tourism—"ecotourism"—to these sites, as already shown in the tropical forest parks of Costa Rica, Ecuador, and Peru, can bring income to remote areas and support jobs, food production, and forest conservation. Elsewhere, many small settlements would be consolidated to make social services easier to provide. Zoning decisions and plans, however, would be made with nature's bent in mind: such concerns as soil quality and drainage would take precedence over traditional ideas about how a city must look.

Dourojeanni, chief of environment at the Inter-American Development Bank, is not a utopian. His message is that, with the right kind of government policies in force, Amazônia can provide a decent livelihood for people *and* maintain biological diversity and climate stability. The key is carefully combining the interests of forestry, mining, and agriculture with those of the millions of "small holders" in the region.

Scattered examples of this approach already exist in the region. In the Peruvian Amazon, for instance, livestock grazing has been combined with forestry and agriculture. Cattle are put into paddocks—two animals per acre—and they eat forest and agricultural waste as food supplements. The upshot is that meat production has increased from 48 pounds per acre per year to 400. Elsewhere, in the Ecuadorian Amazon, pig husbandry has been integrated with agriculture and forestry. Legume trees have been planted in pastureland, with sugarcane and two species of plantain (cooking bananas) nearby. The pigs eat the pasture grass, plantain, and sugarcane, and the trees provide the other plants with nitrogen. After eight years, they are beginning to supply firewood for the farmer.

Development options are also being defined by the region's indigenous peoples. The Coordinating Body of the Indigenous Organizations of the Amazon Basin (COICA) represents 1.2 million Amazonian Indians that federated in 1984 to promote their common perspectives and interests. Like many other partisans of Amazônia, they are interested in small, locally controlled activities. Their vision is to have well-defined native territories where families and communities can get all the food and basic materials they need from the land. "The key to development for us is an extensive, diversified, and integral territory where all its occupants, people, animals, trees, and rivers will share the benefit," states COICA. "The Amazon's wealth lies in its forests; that is what gives life to all of us."

Other environmentally benign development models have been proposed by a group called AIDESEP (the Inter-Ethnic Association for Development of the Peruvian Tropical Forest). These combine the knowledge and skills of indigenous groups with ideas culled from the outside world and adapted over time to local situations. In 1990, AIDESEP invited a group of environmentalists from abroad to its *Huerto Integral Familiar Comunal* project (Family/Community Integrated Garden Project) near Pucalpa, Peru. Twenty years of colonization and cattle ranching had devastated the landscape in Pucalpa, but five years of care is beginning to bring it to life again. Even more impressive, the land was restored without pesticides and without taking the three-month dry-season break from production that other farms in the area do.

According to Bruce Cabarle, a forester from World Resources Institute who was among the foreign visitors, the AIDESEP project has two mainstays. One is the *cama elevada,* or raised bed plot, which is used to restore productivity on abandoned pastures and farmland. No fewer than 42 annual and perennial plants are placed among the trees in such beds. Plantain and yucca are raised for the market, and maize, peppers, tomatoes, sesame, ginger, and other foods are produced for household use. Pole beans and pigeon peas enrich the soil. Trees bear fruit (guava), serve as the base for climbing beans that fix nitrogen in the garden, provide specialty items (palm hearts for salads), and timber (laurel and mahogany).

Cabarle describes the second technique, the *chacra redonda*, or round garden plot, as a "sedentary slash-and-burn" site. Starting with 13 acres or so, the Amerindian farmers clear 2 acres within the forest plot for intensive agriculture, leaving the surrounding 11 acres forested. Within the opening, crops are planted in concentric circles, beginning with vegetables in the center, staples in the second ring, cash crops in the third, fruit trees in the fourth, and timber trees in the outer ring. (This pattern tries to mimic the natural succession of plants from the center of a forest opening out to the forest edge.) Aromatic plants and spices (including marigold and cilantro) are planted to repel insects, and local concoctions of wood ash, worms, leaves, spices, and manures are fermented and applied to ward off pests. Fish are placed in the drainage ditches and water holes to feed on insect eggs.

Backup for these two farming techniques include seed-storage banks, fish ponds with 18 varieties of edible fish, and the production of guinea pigs, geese, ducks, pigeons, and guinea hens for meat. (Cattle, chickens, pigs, and goats are too hard on the environment.) Native family groups receive three months of training, and graduates return to their federations to share what they have learned.

All is not perfect. Training materials are in short supply, and local support for returning graduates leaves something to be desired. Also, there is a legal "catch 22": the forested part of the farm is considered "unproductive vegetative cover" under the law and thus falls into public domain. On the other hand, after just five years, the project has already demonstrated how to reclaim degraded lands, how to maintain forest cover as part of agricultural landscapes, and how farmers can get by without seeking off-farm wages—a necessity when farms shut down during the dry season.

The project has relieved pressure on the forest and has reduced the traditional insecurity felt by families during the arid months. Crop yields are continuing to climb and have already surpassed those of other local farms.

Yet another model for economic development in Amazônia is being backed by the rubber tappers. They want the government to hold title to large tracts of land managed by people who make their living gathering rubber, Brazil nuts, fruits, and other nontimber products of the forest. On these extractive reserves (now being established under law in Brazil on some 10 million acres), forest cover on vast areas can be retained while resident communities get what they need—income and security. Conceptually, this approach can complement the schemes put forth by Dourojeanni and AIDESEP.

Not all of the forest's "extracts" are equally economically viable. Natural rubber extraction is clearly in economic trouble. It takes 700 acres of natural forest to produce the amount of rubber produced by a single acre in a plantation. As Andrew Revkin notes in *The Burning Season: The Murder of Chico Mendes and the Fight for the Amazon Rainforest,* wild rubber is marketable only because Brazil imposes a 200 percent tariff on the superior Asian rubber and forces domestic tire companies to buy the wild product. But the possible decline in the value of wild rubber need not signal the demise of the "extractive reserve." The communities involved are not so much committed to rubber as they are to harvesting the forests' wealth of renewable resources.

EMERGING POLITICAL ALLIANCES

In recent years, Brazil's indigenous peoples have organized themselves to protect their lives and their rain forest home. As their successes multiply, so do episodes of harassment and death threats.

At the forefront of these indigenous peoples' fight have been the Kayapó, 8,500 people comprising a nation of 14 communities located in southern Pará. The Kayapó support themselves by hunting, fishing, farming, and gathering wild plants, of which they use more than 600 species for food, medicine, thatch, oil, paint, dye, fiber, soap, and insect repellent. They keep their small agricultural fields productive for up to 25 years—a stunning technical feat on the area's nutrient-poor forest soils. But their way of life is disappearing. And, as Kayapó leader Paiakan says, "without our culture we cannot survive. Without our culture, there is no reason to live."

According to Terrence Turner, a University of Chicago anthropologist who has worked with the Kayapó for 25 years, these people have "a tradition of political organization and oratory" that has prepared them well for today's deforestation crisis. In the past 6 years, Turner says, the group has organized demonstrations in Brasília, protesting the dumping of radioactive waste on their land, government attempts to deny them free speech, and clauses in Brazil's new constitution that would weaken native rights. They have also driven illegal settlers off their lands and have "recaptured" two gold mines illegally opened in Kayapó territory.

"Every one of the successful Kayapó actions," says Taylor, "was conceived and organized by a remarkable young leader named Paiakan." In early 1988, Paiakan and another Kayapó leader, Kube-i, took their case to Washington, D.C. With the help of American ethnobiologist Darrell Posey, they protested the proposed Altamira Hydroelectric Complex—the most extensive dam system ever planned in Brazil—slated to flood thousands of square miles of Indian forestland along the Xingú River. The largest dam, Babaquara, would have created the biggest artificial lake on earth, flooding 2,000 square miles of forest and displacing 70,000 people. After the meetings, the World Bank decided to postpone its $500-million loan.

When Paiakan, Kube-i, and Posey returned to Brazil, trouble awaited. All three were charged under a law prohibiting political activity by foreigners. If prosecuted and found guilty, each could have faced one to three years in prison and subsequent expulsion from the country. According to Cultural Survival, Amerindians had never before been charged as foreigners in Brazil. When Kube-i showed up for his hearing in the fall of 1988, he brought along some 400 Kayapó warriors dressed in ceremonial clothing. "Fifty shock troops of the military police confronted them at the door of the federal court, in a face-off that made Brazil's front pages," reports *Cultural Survival Quarterly*. "The judge hearing the case refused to let Kube-i into court unless he dressed in 'white man's clothes,' since he considered the Indians' dress 'a sign of disrespect.' " Wide press coverage of these events and tens of thousands of letters of support for the Kayapó from all over the world turned this situation into "an international *cause célèbre* and an embarrassment for the Brazilian government," which dropped the case in February 1989.

An even hotter international press item appeared that same month: in Altamira, 600 Amerindians gathered to protest the construction of the Xingú River dam complex and helped to kill the World Bank funding for it—for the moment anyway. As Nicholas Hildyard reported in *The Ecologist,* the Indians listened "patiently as José Antônio Muniz Lopes, the chief engineer of Brazil's electricity conglomerate, *Electronorte,* smoothly outlined his case for building a massive hydroelectric scheme on the Xingú river." When he was finished, "600 Indians rose as one, raising their arrows and clubs in protest and chanting their disapproval."

Nearly 40 groups from 26 Indian nations made it to the Altamira meeting. According to Hildyard, this showing made it the largest gathering of Indians in modern times. It also may have been historic. As Cultural Survival's Jason Clay puts it, these "traditional enemies have decided to bury the hatchet because they know their new enemies are more dangerous than their old ones."

A month after the Altamira meeting, a new coalition called "Peoples of the Forest" came into being. In March 1989, rubber tappers, Amerindians, and other forest dwellers met in Rio Branco, capital of Acre, to make common cause against ranchers, miners, and loggers. "There were old hatreds still smoldering," write Susanna Hecht and Alexander Cockburn in *The Nation.* "Indians remembered relatives pushed from their land by agents of the rubber barons, with uncles killed and sisters raped. Rubber tappers remembered Indian raids." But today both groups are losing their lives and their land to the same destructive forces, so they are banding together to fight what they see as the common enemy.

The embryonic coalition met again in April 1989. They called for economic development models that respect their cultures and traditions, a say about government projects on land they inhabit, and the creation of extractive reserves, among other concessions. So far, "Peoples of the Forest" is too small and too disorganized to have much clout, but if its constituent groups get better organized it could become a powerful force.

One potentially great influence on the fate of the forest has been the emergence of a strong coalition of native forest dwellers. COICA sponsored a well-attended international summit meeting of indigenous peoples and environmentalists in Iquitos, Peru, in May 1990. The agenda released there, the Iquitos Declaration, states "that the recognition of territories for indigenous peoples, to develop programs of management and conservation, is an essential alternative for the future of the Amazon." Signed by all groups present, the declaration calls for an "Indigenous and Environmentalist Alliance for an Amazon for Humanity."

COICA provided professionally prepared statements of its agenda for the bilateral and multilateral funders of Amazon development, the international community, and environmentalists. For the first time, the native communities articulated in no uncertain terms how they want to see development approaches in the Amazon change. They expect nothing less than full participation in the dialogue, planning, and execution of all projects that will affect their territories. They also want to be involved with the non-Amerindian communities in formulating new development options that don't "spew petroleum in the rivers, benefit a minority of elites and persecute local inhabitants."

STRAWS IN THE WIND?

In late 1989, Colombia's President Virgilio Barco announced that "land and indigenous peoples belong to each other" and turned over a vast Amazonian tract to indigenous inhabitants, setting in motion a policy shift that he hopes other Amazonian nations will emulate. Barco has come to believe that Amazônia can't be protected unless indigenous people control it and that, if what the Amazonian states really want is to promote the rational use of the Amazon, they should begin by ending colonization.

Recognizing the interest of indigenous peoples in safeguarding the forest far into the future, Colombia has granted them inalienable rights to more than 26 million acres of Amazonian tropical forest. If plans go forward to grant another 13 million acres along the border with Brazil, writes Peter Bunyard in *The Ecologist,* "Some 200,000 indigenous people will have land rights over an area the size of Great Britain." This move was not simple benevolence on the part of the Colombian government. What was known unofficially for years was finally recognized officially—that the government was simply unable to manage the territory and that colonization schemes were a failure.

Brazil's new Collor administration has also raised new expectations and cautious optimism about Brazil's portion of the Amazon Basin. Collor has appointed respected environmentalists to two key positions—José Lutzenberger as minister of the environment and José Goldemberg as science and technology advisor. The industrial subsidies and perks for cattle ranchers that tended to promote deforestation have been eliminated, and agricultural investments will now be taxed as part of Collor's economic reform. According to Steve Schwartzman of the Environmental Defense Fund, "taxing agriculture will not reverse the concentration of landholdings, a major underlying cause of deforestation and land conflicts, but it could stop it from increasing."

Hopes for further concrete action brightened in 1989, when Brazil and the other Amazon Basin countries together created an Environment Commission (CEMA) to coordinate conservation and development efforts in the region. Under this new plan, each country has a specific job to do: Brazil is to inventory flora and fauna while Venezuela analyzes biodiversity and tribal groups, Peru studies hydrobiological resources, Bolivia weighs legislation, and Colombia assesses management of protected areas.

At the same time, international concern about the Amazon is heightening. In January 1989, delegates from tropical countries and leading industrial nations endorsed a European Community proposal for a World Forest Conservation Protocol. Along with international trade deals and financial assistance to tropical countries, this grand bargain, to be negotiated as part of the Global Climate Convention now under discussion, is expected to cover the planning, use, replanting, and protection of rain forests. A year later, scientists, government officials, and other Amazonian specialists from the region and abroad met in Manaus to analyze the status of every major plant and animal group in Amazônia and to computer-map the sites of greatest biological value with future permanent protection in mind. The final communique from the July 1990 Summit meeting of the seven leading industrial nations pledged support for development of a new international agreement to preserve the world's forests by 1992. While the contents of such an agreement have yet to be worked out, the potential for making forests a higher political priority and for prompting conservation and sustainable use is exciting.

New alliances among Amazonian forest dwellers are also heartening, as are first steps toward environmentally sound economic development by President Collor and other leaders in the region and heightened international interest in Amazônia's forests and people. Still, tragic conflicts remain. As Philip Bennett writes, "the destruction of the rain forest is driven by individual struggles for both survival and wealth. The flames are fanned by dramatic social conflicts: between rich and poor, Indians and pioneers, those with too much land and those with none." Wealthy cattle ranchers and corporate logging and mining companies appear as Goliaths to local peoples. But, at the same time, many other forest invaders are themselves hopelessly poor: a single photograph of an open-pit gold mine brimming with half-clad workers like a cauldron about to boil over makes it plain enough that nobody on the safe side of desperation would toil in social isolation in the blazing heat, much less brave mercury poisoning.

Misery describes the lives of Brazil's underclass outside Amazônia's forests, too. Although some have been the object of assistance programs, many of these people have received even less publicity, moral support, and financial help than the indigenous peoples fighting to preserve their way of life, and growing numbers of poor people have overwhelmed government efforts to provide education, sanitation, housing, and other necessities. For those stuck in squatter settlements or barely making a go of it as farm laborers, Amazônia's land, minerals, water, and timber will remain a draw; their environmental perspective is bound to differ from preservationists crying "hands off the Amazon!"

This combination of entrenched interests and demeaning poverty—typical of many tropical countries—will continue until the social and institutional forces behind both human and forest impoverishment are met head on. The sound new approaches being tried offer hope, and the power of government policies to continue the cycle of destruction can be redirected to stimulate "greener" economic development. The losses to people and nature are already great, but it's not too late to change course.

4

Other Tropical Forests under Siege

All the evidence suggests that nature
consists of perfectly attuned linkages
stretching out of our sight—and out of our
understanding—in all directions. Yet, we
imagine we can destroy this forest and build
another.

> DAVID KELLY AND GARY BRAASCH
> *Secrets of the Old Growth Forest*

Think of tropical forests, and *Amazon* is probably the first region—or word—that comes to mind. Yet, nearly one-third of the world's tropical forests are in Africa, Asia, and other parts of Latin America. Even the United States has tropical forests—in Puerto Rico, Hawaii, Guam, American Samoa, and the U.S. Virgin Islands.

A quick tour through just a few of these other tropical regions can help us gauge deforestation's true extent, see how the local causes of forest loss differ, and get a sense of how the lives of people who depend directly on forests change when the deforestation rate quickens. In the portraits that follow, similarities between forests stand out and give us some sense of the global dimensions of deforestation and forest degradation. Important differences that reflect each country's unique culture, biological endowment, and economy also emerge, and learning to respect these is essential to making headway against the global deforestation crisis.

THE U.S. TROPICS

Tropical forests in Puerto Rico and Hawaii make up less than 1 percent of the world's total. But these scattered patches of paradise contain many unique species and ecosystems—some of them under siege. And they are home to people whose lives depend upon the economic goods and environmental services of their forest.

Discovered by Christopher Columbus in 1493, Puerto Rico's 2 million acres were once almost entirely blanketed by forest. By the late 1940s, just 6 percent of the island remained forested. Since then, forests have been growing back. Vast areas of the island were abandoned during World War II as rural inhabitants immigrated in droves to the continent. By 1985, forest cover reached 675,000 acres, established mostly on abandoned pasture and coffee lands and on once-eroded hillsides. Today, about 4 percent of Puerto Rico, or 34,000 acres, is protected in either national or commonwealth forests that contain representative samples of the island's mountain, dry mangrove, rain forest, and other forest environments.

Puerto Rico's rich flora and fauna have long been a tourist draw. Many of these colorful species are endemic: 300 of the island's 3,000 species are found nowhere else on Earth. One-quarter of the Commonwealth's 547 tree species are unique to Puerto Rico, as are 12 of its 232 native bird species. In all, Puerto Rico has as many tree species as the entire continental United States.

While it's cheering to know that Puerto Rico's forests are recovering, especially in federal and state forest reserves, nagging concerns linger. The island's varied mountain, coastal, and limestone environments provide sanctuary for hundreds of endemic species, of which 27 are "very endangered," 29 are "endangered," and another 15 are borderline. Any habitat loss in these regions means species loss. Damage to water supplies is at issue, too: as forest cover is stripped from mountain watersheds to make way for urban expansion and tourism development, aquifers are depleted, stream flows change, and wells dry up. So, although Puerto Rico's forests are on the mend, their health and longevity can't be taken for granted.

In Hawaii—what one scientist calls the "jewel in the crown" of our nation's plant and animal diversity—the record is also mixed, and the fate of even more species is hanging in the balance.

Some 2,500 miles from the nearest continent, Hawaii is made up of the world's most isolated group of oceanic islands. Few plants or animals had the qualities needed to survive migration to these lands so distant from the continent. But those that did gave rise to an astonishing variety of new species, each specifically adapted to one of Hawaii's many unique habitats.

Born in volcanic activity, the islands have extremely rugged surfaces that provide diverse mini-habitats—each with its own microclimate and each separated from the others by rough and sometimes craggy terrain. According to a 1989 report of the Natural Resources Defense Council, *Extinction in Paradise,* "the range in rainfall alone is staggering, from 300–400 inches per year on the mountain tops—including Mount Waialeale where the annual rainfall of 460 inches is the world's highest—to 10 to 20 inches per year on the leeward sides of the islands. Extreme differences can be found within an hour's walk." On Kauai's famed Na Pali Coast, for instance, each turn a hiker makes along the many fingers of land that jut into the ocean can bring a new spectacle—first guava trees, then tall grasses, then sea-washed caves.

The combination of Hawaii's geographic and climatic diversity and its long isolation has given rise to an explosive evolution of new species on these isles. Each varied site, with unique mixes of soil, rainfall, and sunlight patterns, and natural barriers to contact with neighboring sites, creates the opportunity for nature to "select" different qualities of the original plant and animal immigrants. For example, an estimated 270 original flowering plant species have developed into more than 1,000 species today. From an estimated 300 to 400 colonizing insects, about 10,000 species have evolved. Some of these can be listed among the world's strangest, including meat-eating caterpillars that resemble leaves, twigs, mosses, and forest rubble. (Meat to a caterpillar, incidentally, is spiders and other insects.) One wingless cricket that biologists believe can survive long voyages across the open sea lives only in the wave splash zone of rocky seacoasts. Another cricket species makes its home on lava flows, and two are blind cave dwellers.

Similar diversity can be seen among Hawaii's 20 honeycreeper species. Each of these birds feeds on a different food and has evolved a highly distinctive bill for getting at the right seed, insect, or nectar. But the most diverse of Hawaii's organisms are the islands' 800 or more *Drosophila* fruit flies, which represent perhaps a fourth of all the world's species of this common fly. Overall, scientists say, more than 95 percent of Hawaii's native species live nowhere else—a record unmatched anywhere else on Earth.

The long isolation that allowed life in Hawaii to assume so many unique forms over millions of years has also made these species highly vulnerable. Unlike most continental plants, Hawaiian species evolved in a world comparatively free of pests and predators. As a result, these "innocent" plants have no thorns, spines, or other defenses against being eaten and trampled. By the same token, many now-extinct Hawaiian birds built their nests on open ground instead of in the safety of trees. One bird, the Hawaiian goose or nene, even lost the ability to fly.

As soon as people arrived on the islands, Hawaiian plants and animals began to take a beating. At least 45 species of land birds died out during the Polynesians' 1,000-year occupation. But the last two centuries, writes entomologist Wayne C. Gagné of Hawaii's Bishop Museum, have been far harder on the native biota.

This war on species and forests has been one of attrition. Colonists cut down nearly all of Hawaii's lowland tropical forests to make way for sheep and cattle pastures or for sugarcane and pineapple plantations. More recently, forests have been cleared to make room for resorts, housing, and geothermal energy development. Forests have also fallen victim to the foreign plants and animals that the colonists brought with them: "More than 2,000 alien arthropods [insects mainly], 50 alien land birds, and 18 alien mammals [have now been] established," writes Gagné. Roughly 900 introduced species of plants now nearly outnumber Hawaii's native flora, and today only about one-quarter of Hawaii's land area remains in anything close to its natural state.

Pets, rats, and farm animals brought in from outside have wreaked havoc on the islands' fragile and defenseless native species. The introduced pigs, goats, and sheep have run wild for decades, eating, trampling, and uprooting the native vegetation. Aggressive introduced plants invade these sites. With chemical warfare, thorns, and other bodily defense mechanisms, these new colonizers can resist plant-eating mammals. Introduced egg-eating rodents and other mammalian predators killed off virtually all the islands' flightless birds. Unfortunately, the obvious message hasn't sunk in: exotic species are still being introduced, both deliberately and accidentally. According to Gagné, about 20 foreign insect species make it to the islands each year, and "human efforts to right the biotic wrongs have resulted in some serious blunders": the mongoose wiped out the remaining flightless rails instead of the rodents it was brought in to control, and carnivorous snails imported to do battle with the giant African snail prey on native land molluscs instead.

Today, nearly 40 percent of all Hawaii's known endemic bird species have become extinct. Nearly three-quarters of the remaining bird species are threatened or endangered, as are 40 percent of Hawaii's native plants. Although Hawaii makes up less than 0.2 percent of the United States' total land area, it is home to more than one-quarter of all U.S. endangered species—and to nearly three-quarters of the nation's recorded extinctions.

To protect more species and to keep imported species out of national parks, both state and federal governments have recently given Hawaii more of the attention it deserves. Congress has provided nearly $20 million since 1984 to purchase and protect the forests where Hawaii's endangered birds live. Private organizations are also getting into the act. In 1988, the MacArthur Foundation granted more than $3.5 million to five conservation organizations working in Hawaii to step up education programs, research, and advocacy, and to buy land containing key habitats so as to preserve them. Yet, according to a 1990 study by the Natural Resources Defense Council, the combined budget of the Fish and Wildlife Service and the National Park Service in Hawaii is only one-sixth of what is needed to keep habitats intact in Hawaii's eight national wildlife refuges and four national parks.

In Hawaii, conservationists use the same arguments for saving tropical forests as they do elsewhere. Forests help maintain watersheds, soils, coastal resources, and biological diversity. But in Hawaii the diversity of life forms means that the stakes are particularly high. If that great wealth isn't respected, we might someday lose the real Hawaii, which is far more beautiful and ecologically complex than just its sun, surf, and sand.

AFRICAN EXTREMES

Today Africa still conjures up images of breathtaking landscapes, diverse cultures, and mystery. But the colonial powers superimposed their political system and cultural values upon the native societies. Colonial plantation agriculture, timber harvesting, and other economic activities transformed much of the original landscape, and the human suffering and natural resource devastation that stem from colonization live on.

Examples abound. The introduction of European cattle herds into areas that had natural grasslands has contributed to overgrazing of habitats that once supported diverse wildlife. While the natural plant and animal communities could withstand Africa's repeated dry periods and the continent's many wild ungulates could forage on various types of vegetation and survive dry spells, domestic cattle need succulent plants and large quantities of water. Bringing in cattle thus exaggerated the hardships of the dry periods and contributed to "desertification"—gradual devegetation that occurs when soils are laid bare to sun and wind. (In extreme cases, dunes form, making it all but impossible for forests and grasslands to recover.) Similarly, the emphasis since colonial times on export crops, including cotton, nuts, palm oil, coffee, and cacao, means that the region's best soils are dedicated to crops that neither feed nor employ many local people.

Even after colonialism officially ended, independent governments continued to produce crops and timber for international markets to earn foreign funds to pay for development programs and to pay off growing national debts. To this, add rapid population growth, and the net result is rising pressure to clear new lands for food production and to harvest fuelwood for domestic heating and cooking.

This combination of human and natural pressures on the people and their environment has damaged millions of Africans' hold on life. Worried about how they will make it from day to day, they have no choice but to put off any so-called long-term planning. Societies that have lived peacefully with and revered wildlife are forced by the demands of survival to collaborate in the international market for such totems as gorillas, rhinos, and elephants. These same pressures have forced many rural Africans to clear more forestland or to return to idled land sooner than they know they should. As Marius Jacobs writes in *The Tropical Rain Forest: A First Encounter*, "man became the deadly enemy of the rain forest when the whites . . . organized large-scale settled agriculture, plantations, and timber exploitation. When roads and bridges were built, this made the forest even more accessible and vulnerable. In this century, man has so violently attacked the natural vegetation of Africa that it has justly been named 'the devastated continent.' "

Despite this onslaught, Africa still claims 500 million acres of tropical forest, nearly 20 percent of the world's total. Although deforestation's causes differ markedly from country to country, commercial logging, subsistence agriculture (often catalyzed by logging), and fuelwood gathering take the worst toll on the continent. In West Africa, deforestation is rampant; since 1975, deforestation there has been nearly four times the global average, according to resource economist Malcolm Gillis. One west African country, the Ivory Coast, has the dubious distinction of having the world's highest national deforestation rate, about 5 percent a year. According to Gillis, the Ivory Coast's forest cover in 1985 was less than one-fifth of what it had been in 1900. (On an absolute scale, though, 15 times more land is deforested every year in Brazil.)

In contrast to the Ivory Coast, Central African countries still boast vast areas of tropical forest, mainly because the human population in this region is sparse and mostly urban, and the forests are relatively inaccessible. About two-thirds of the region's forests have scarcely even been disturbed. In Gabon on Africa's central western coast, for example, the deforestation rate is only 0.1 percent—one of the world's lowest.

What has saved Gabon's forests so far? First, thanks to Gabon's rich mineral deposits, citizens enjoy one of Africa's highest standards of living, so farmers aren't forced to turn to the forests.

Second, Gabon's economy is centered on mining and manufacturing, so pressure to log the forest is low. And, recently,
the country's government has begun to recognize how important
conservation is to the nation's continued economic development.

Gabon features one of Africa's most diverse forests. According
to Thomas 0. McShane of the World Wildlife Fund, the country's
tropical forests contain 8,000 species of plants, 600 of birds, and
over 150 of mammals, including rare lowland gorillas and chimpan-
zees, in addition to 17 other primate species. Gabon also is Africa's
greatest sanctuary for elephants, which is particularly significant
in view of the slaughter taking place elsewhere to serve the international ivory trade.

In *Orion* magazine, Louise H. Emmons of the Smithsonian
Institution and The American Museum of Natural History de-
scribed the diversity of one group of somewhat less charismatic
animals—squirrels—in a forest that she studied in Gabon. "A
North American forest has one to three [types of] squirrels,"
Emmons writes. "There were nine of them in that Gabon forest.
How do they all manage to live together in one forest?" After
completing her research, Emmons found out: each of the nine is
a different size, and for the most part each eats different foods.
Thus, competition is minimal, since, while some species feed on
nuts, fruits, and insects in the canopy, others only touch these
foods once they've hit the forest floor. To support this peaceable
community of squirrel species, Emmon says, "a forest must have
a great many species of trees and lianas [rope plants], each producing fruit in its own rhythm. . . ."

Can a country so rich in forest wealth hold the line against the
pressures that have all but destroyed the natural forest resources
of some other African nations? In the past, the population of
central African countries remained remarkably low relative to that
of the rest of the continent. But it is now shooting up rapidly—about 3 percent a year. At this rate, Gabon and its neighbors
will have four times as many people a century from now as they
do today. Compounding the pressures on natural resources, new
roads are also opening up forests. And, in Gabon, the prices of

some of the country's most important exports—petroleum, natural gas, manganese, and uranium—have recently fallen, leaving timber a tempting source of quick cash.

Since Gabon does not have a sea of rural poor waiting to invade its forests, commercial logging operations there probably won't bring waves of new settlers as they have in other tropical regions. But this country, and Central Africa in general, do face another serious threat to forests: commercial game hunting. Very little livestock is raised in Central Africa, and its people derive nearly all of their daily protein from wild game and fish. City dwellers have created a strong market for bush meat, so it commands high prices. As a result, commercial hunters, by and large unregulated by their governments, track and kill tremendous numbers of forest animals. According to McShane, a ton of bush meat arrives in one town, Libreville, every week. For the meat trade, new logging roads mean access to once-impenetrable forests. For forest-dwelling animals, they can mean wholesale slaughter.

If wildlife hunting expands, important seed-dispersing species could easily become endangered. Trees that depend upon these species could eventually disappear from parts of the region. For example, in the Ivory Coast alone, elephants disperse the seeds of 37 tree species, only 7 of which have back-up carriers. If elephants die out, so will 30 kinds of trees. In some forests where elephants have already disappeared, only the older trees of certain species can be found. It will only be a matter of time, according to Emmons, before the adult trees and all the animals that depended on *them*, including two of the squirrels Emmons studied, will be gone, too. "Who would have thought," she writes, "that when the elephants disappear from the African rain forest, thirty major tree species could go with them, as well as the two giant squirrels that live on seeds of these species, and who can tell what else?" And who knows exactly how *people* will be affected by breaks in the food chain and rips in the very fabric of forest ecosystems?

The African country with the most forest to lose—some 260 million acres of closed forest—is Zaire. This country boasts almost half of the remaining forest in Africa, more than five times as much as the second-place holder, Gabon. But the country's fast-growing rural population and the prominence of slash-and-burn agriculture contribute to a high annual deforestation rate of 990 million acres. So does the fact that 85 percent of the country's energy comes from fuelwood.

Thanks more to inaccessibility than to public policy, Zaire's forests have remained largely untouched by the commercial chain saw. Perhaps 35 to 70 million cubic feet of timber are commercially harvested annually, compared to 1,225 million cubic feet for fuelwood. But, with Zaire's increased need for foreign exchange to repay debts that financed development projects and with the rising prices of timber, how long can these rich forests and the people and other species they house last?

Zaire's current forest management and conservation efforts are tied closely to the Tropical Forestry Action Plan, an initiative designed to help developing countries save, manage, and harvest their forests in sustainable ways. But making the plan work is no easy task. Robert Winterbottom, a specialist in African forestry at World Resources Institute, sums up Zaire's challenge like this: "the resources base is immense, the economic and political problems are difficult, if not acute, debt burdens are severe, and the rural and institutional infrastructure is crumbling." Zaire's Department of Land Affairs, Environment, and Nature Conservation has a program for taking care of Zaire's forestlands, but a lack of well-trained staff, operating funds, and coordination limit the program's potential.

Right now, the fate of Zaire's forest probably hinges on financial and technical support from international organizations. So far, outside assistance has been quite generous, and world interest is likely to at least hold steady too, partly because Zaire's forests contain nearly a third of Sub-Saharan Africa's "carbon inventory." The 17 billion tons of carbon "sequestered" in the nation's forests could be critical in international efforts to slow global climate change, and Zaire has plenty of room to plant more trees, too. Yet, current efforts are slow. With a reforestation/deforestation ratio of around 1:150, Zaire lags far behind the worldwide average of 1:10.

SOUTHEAST ASIA—CHAIN SAW AND TORCH

Asia contains about 650 million acres of tropical forest, almost a fourth of the world's total. But, between 1976 and 1980, more than 4 million acres of these rich rain forests were cleared *each year*. As in some parts of Africa, deforestation in this region stems mainly from commercial logging: four-fifths of all tropical hardwood exports come from Asia. But the expansion of market-oriented agriculture and the spread of land-colonization programs also take a sizable toll on the forest.

Indonesia harbors over half of Asia's remaining tropical forests. More than 40 percent of the country is forested, especially in Kalimantan, Sumatra, and Irian Jaya. Indonesian forests are also Asia's greatest repositories of plant and animal species. With Malaysia running a close second, Indonesia is Asia's richest country in plant diversity. Blessed with more than 20,000 flowering plant species, it ranks close to Latin America's most botanically well-endowed countries. The country's mammals are also the world's most diverse, and more than a third of its 515 mammal species are unique to Indonesia. It also has more parrots and swallowtail butterfly species than any other country.

But Indonesia's species-rich forests are falling fast to the chain saw. In *Public Policies and the Misuse of Forest Resources*, Malcolm Gillis says that between 1950 and 1985 the country lost some 98 million acres of closed-canopy forest. He believes another 2.3 million acres may be disappearing each year. The pace of logging is so dizzying today that some experts predict that many of the most valuable commercial forests will be completely "logged out" in the next few years. Outside of protected areas, virtually all of Indonesia's lumber-rich forests have already been carved up into logging concessions. Some local people get jobs as a result, but the profits revert to the owners of the concessions and, in many cases, their foreign partners. Rarely do profits from logging reach the government treasury, let alone local communities.

Indonesia reaps sorely needed revenue from its forests ($2.8 billion in export earnings in fiscal year 1988–89, of which $350 million were estimated as coming from royalties and fees). But Malcolm Gillis calls the benefits of commercial logging "check-

OUR TROPICAL CONNECTION

Think of many of the things we take for granted: hot coffee, a banana for lunch, an apple pie fragrant with cinnamon and nutmeg, a chocolate candy bar, a rubber ball, latex paint to touch up the walls, or anesthesia to ease the pain of surgery. Ingredients in all of these come from tropical forests. Indeed, the array of everyday products that tropical forests provide is astonishing. Here are some items these forests supply.

Woods	Houseplants	Spices
Teak	*Anthurium*	Allspice
Mahogany	Croton	Black pepper
Rosewood	*Dieffenbachia*	Cardamom
Balsa	*Dracaena*	Cayenne
Sandalwood	Fiddle-leaf fig	Chili
	Mother-in-law's	Cinnamon
Used for:	tongue	Cloves
Toys	Parlor ivy	Ginger
Doors	*Philodendron*	Mace
Windowsills	Rubber tree plant	Nutmeg
Flooring	*Schefflera*	Paprika
Paneling	Silver vase	Sesame seeds
Veneer	bromeliad	Turmeric
Cabinetry	*Spathiphyllum*	Vanilla
Dresser drawers	Swiss cheese plant	
Salad bowls	Zebra plant	
Garden funiture		
Packing cases		
and boxes		
Insulation		
Railroad ties		
Wharf pilings		
Boat building		
Chemical vats		
Buoyancy material		
Drawing boards		

(*continued*)

OUR TROPICAL CONNECTION   *(continued)*

Fruits

Avocado
Banana
Coconut
Grapefruit
Lemon
Lime
Mango
Orange
Papaya
Passion fruit
Pineapple
Plantain
Tangerine

Vegetables and Other Foods

Brazil nuts
Cane sugar
Cashew nuts
Chocolate
Coffee
Cucumber
Hearts of palm
Macadamia nuts
Manioc/tapioca
Mayonnaise (coconut oil)
Okra
Peanuts
Peppers
Soft drinks (cola)
Tea
Vermouth (cascarilla oil)

Fibers and Their Uses

Bamboo (furniture, baskets)
Jute/kenaf (rope, burlap)
Kapok (insulation, soundproofing, life jackets)
Raffia (rope, cord, baskets)
Ramie (cotton-ramie fabric, fishing line)
Rattan (furniture, wickerwork, baskets, chair seats)

Oils and Their Uses

Bay oil (perfume)
Camphor oil (perfume, soap, disinfectant, detergent)
Cascarilla oil (confections, beverages)
Coconut oil (suntan lotion, candles)
Eucalyptus oil (perfume, cough drops)

(continued)

OUR TROPICAL CONNECTION   (*continued*)

Guaic oil (perfume)
Oil of star anise (scenting, confections, beverages, cough drops)
Palm oil (shampoo, detergents)
Patchouli oil (perfume)
Rosewood oil (perfume, cosmetics, flavoring)
Sandalwood oil (perfume)
Tolu balsam oil (confections, soaps, cosmetics, cough drops)
Ylang-ylang (perfume)

Gums, Resins, and Their Uses

Chicle latex (chewing gum)
Copaiba (perfume, fuel)
Copal (paints and varnishes)
Gutta percha (golf ball covers)
Rubber latex (rubber products)
Tung oil (wood finishing)

Pharmaceuticals and Their Uses

Annatto (red dye)
Curare (muscle relaxant for surgery)
Diosgenin (sex hormones, birth control pills, steroids, asthma and arthritis treatment)
Quassia (insecticide)
Quinine (antimalarial, pneumonia treatment)
Reserpine (sedative, tranquilizer)
Strophanthus (heart disease)
Strychnine (emetic, stimulant)

Source: Tropical Rainforests: A Disappearing Treasure (Smithsonian Institution, Washington, D.C., Traveling Exhibition Service, 1988).

ered at the very best." And, he adds, "the social and environmental costs of forest despoilation are becoming more apparent with each passing year." Indeed, the cost of raw logs and the price of timber products do not include the growing bill associated with displaced forest residents, soil erosion, river siltation, and loss of key watersheds. That cost will have to be borne by Indonesians and their heirs.

As a fellow for the Institute of Current World Affairs, Judith Mayer witnessed some of the social costs of logging firsthand in several small villages in East Kalimantan. "At first, almost no one on the banks of the Lawa [River] took any notice of the logging companies' arrival," Mayer writes. "By mid-1984, villagers along the river had begun to connect new logging operations in the river's catchment area to the Lawa's strange new behavior. As one village chief put it, 'In 1983 and 1984, many of us here believed the river had changed because of a solar eclipse in June 1983. But that was not the cause. Since 1983, there is just less to hold the water at the river head. The forest is cut and rain leaks away too fast. The river floods, then dries up. And it is always muddy.' "

On a local level, the once-clear river's heavy load of silt makes daily life a little harder and more bitter. According to Mayer, "boiled river water makes an unappetizing though marginally sanitary drink, and food cooked in the silty water tastes dirty . . . [and] women find that clothing will not come clean in the river water. Dry laundry is permeated with fine brown powder that must be shaken or beaten out."

Brown laundry may be the least of logging's legacies. In late 1982 and early 1983, huge forest fires raged throughout Indonesia's East Kalimantan and Malaysia's Sabah, destroying nearly 9 million acres of Indonesian forest (an area almost the size of Connecticut and Vermont combined) and about half that amount in Sabah. The fires were set by shifting cultivators trying to clear more land. The drought-stricken logged-over forests turned out to be tinderboxes. At base, it was commercial logging's damage to these forests that turned them into the disasters they became. According to Gillis, both droughts and fires have plagued the region since at least the 1800s, when records of such events were first kept. But never before has the country witnessed fires as big and as destructive as the ones that occurred in the early 1980s.

This four-month blaze—almost ten times greater than the fire that swept through Yellowstone in 1988—eventually covered over 13,000 square miles. According to Gillis, "the unlogged [virgin] forest suffered only very light fire damage. The logged-over forest, in the words of one observer, 'went up like a torch.' " (Logging debris is a firetrap, and humidity is lower in logged forests.) The nation lost timber resources equal to four years of exports, Gillis says, "along with tens of millions of dollars of renewable nonwood forest products vital to local residents." Populations of at least two species of hornbills—large fruit-eating forest birds that play a critical role in the regeneration of many forest plants—as well as countless plants, small animals, and insects also died out.

Experts warn that Indonesia's exerience may foretell worse things to come. "The East Kalimantan fires may be a dismaying harbinger for tropical rain forests in many areas where extensive logging and agricultural expansion have taken place," writes Cynthia Mackie in the *Borneo Research Bulletin*. As for the costs to local people, more and more villagers are making the connections among deforestation, "natural" disasters, and loss of their livelihoods, but many simply don't know how to break the chain of cause and effect.

Reflecting on the place of Lawa River people in a new scheme of things, Bu Maryam, an old Suakong woman, had this to say to Judith Mayer: "We used to be the only ones here, so we were big. Now there are the others, the companies. They came. They'll leave, and we'll still be here. We tend to forget about them most of the time, and they forget about us. But they have changed the earth all around us, and suddenly we are small. We must think of what we want for our own future, or those others will make plans for us. We will not know what they are until it is too late. . . ."

This Suakong woman's lament is stinging, but the Thai people may be suffering even more from deforestation. In late 1988, heavy rains hit Thailand's deforested mountains with a vengeance, causing disastrous floods throughout southern Thailand. Reporting from the worst-hit province, Nakhon Si Thammarat, Colin Nickerson wrote in *The Boston Globe*: "The rains fell unusually hard last fall, and mountainsides washed away. Whole villages vanished in the landslides, mudflows, and roiling floodwaters; 460 people died, by official account; thousands were left homeless."

After the flood, Thailand became the first developing nation to ban commercial logging indefinitely. But the official ban came late and has reportedly been violated often. "There is a Thai saying that fences are erected only after the buffaloes are stolen—an apt metaphor for this belated call for remedial action," writes Paisal Sricharatchanya in the *Far Eastern Economic Review*. He may be right. While forests covered an estimated two-thirds of the nation in 1950, today the figure is closer to one-fifth.

Other observers say commercial logging may not have been the only—or even the major—culprit in Thailand's deforestation. Many of the nation's mountain watersheds have been cleared to make way for huge commercial rubber plantations and for subsistence farming, they say, and a logging ban will block neither. Further, some believe that logging bans are ineffective; they say that raising the demand for, and price of, timber is a surefire way to *accelerate* deforestation. Compounding these problems is accelerating timber harvesting in neighboring Burma and Laos to meet continuing Thai demand. Quite possibly, then, the so-called ban is just a sign that Thailand is commercially "logged out"—and a sign to look elsewhere for wood.

Whether or not commercial logging is mainly to blame for southern Thailand's flooding, deforestation itself is doubtless a major cause. Similar disasters have struck throughout Asia, particularly in the lowlands surrounding the denuded Himalayan watershed. In Thailand's Nakhon Si Thammarat, Nickerson talked to Prachuab Saensawant, who lost his farm and all his possessions in the 1988 flood. "I have known floods, but never a flood like this," Saensawant told Nickerson. "They say so many trees were cut from the mountains that the earth could not hold together. If this is true, then those who have taken our forests should be called criminals."

THE COMMON THREAD

As this quick tour of some major tropical forests makes clear, many of the world's rain forests are at risk, and each region faces somewhat different challenges. In Africa, while commercial agriculture and logging drive deforestation in some countries, fuelwood cutting and the need for land to support a burgeoning population lead the siege in others. In Southeast Asia, commercial logging is the primary cause, followed by land-settlement efforts and plantation agriculture. Brazil's deforestation problem stems mainly from economic development programs and settlement schemes designed to earn foreign exchange, settle frontiers, and create homes and employment for the region's millions of landless. Cattle ranching, both industrial and smallscale mining, road construction, and dam building are the most obvious forces of deforestation.

In the United States, the causes of deforestation and the prognosis for the nation's forest wealth are a bit different because poverty is not a driving force. Air pollution from industry, automobiles, and energy production degrades vast areas of land. As the epilogue to this book makes clear, the last remaining old-growth trees are being harvested to provide revenue for corporations and communities and jobs for people who live near forests. Prospects for the recovery of Puerto Rico's tropical forests and endemic species look good, but Hawaii's flora and fauna remain particularly vulnerable to fast-paced urbanization.

A common thread weaves through these regional portraits. In much of the forested world, governments sell off forest resources to promote desperately needed economic development, while the greed of a few, the poverty of many, and population growth all combine to frustrate even the best-laid plans. Too often, forests are poorly managed or simply treated as obstructions to development, and those who decide how the forest will be used too often disregard the rights, perspectives, and knowledge of forest dwellers.

No stroke of genius by a forestry agency or massive forestry investment project can save the forests, because the root causes of deforestation lie outside forestry agency mandates and beyond forest boundaries. In this sense, forests are a litmus test of the competence of governments and of their commitment to economically equitable, socially just, and ecologically sound development. By any honest accounting, trees stand for far more than themselves.

What Can Governments Do?

Restoring, conserving, protecting natural
resources: these are all essential if future
generations are to have a chance to meet
their needs. But if more is not done to meet
the needs of those here today—the majority
of humanity, pushed into over-farming,
over-grazing, over-cutting, even over-
populating, as they look to their children for
extra hands to work and some comfort in
the future—if more is not done for these
people, the earth will be no better off.

LINDA STARKE
Signs of Hope: Working towards Our
Common Future

Global deforestation's scale is immense—each year a tract the size
of Minnesota disappears—and its causes are many and complex.
Scientists and citizens can act to help slow the rate of decline, but
their efforts will be swamped unless governments in developing
countries (where 80 percent of all tropical forests are found) and
in industrial countries (where debt is held and a disproportionate
share of tropical products are consumed) get increasingly serious
about curbing deforestation, too.

Theoretically, the wealthy industrial nations of the temperate
zone should have little trouble stemming forest losses at home.
Their soils and forest ecosystems are relatively forgiving, and
their economies and social systems are not crippled by foreign
debt and widespread poverty. But the policy reform needed to
save their own forests and to help save those in the tropics has
comparatively high political and economic costs and is often gov-
erned by the number of votes such changes will earn politicians.
In a word, the needed changes won't come easily.

In the tropical countries, efforts to control forest destruction will be harder still. The inexorable links between deforestation and migration, people's growing alienation from their natural resource base, and government policies that promote forest clearing and degradation can be indirect, hidden, or politically charged. And poverty and population growth compound the difficulties of every effort to put people and resources on a sustainable footing.

Tough challenges all, but history does afford some precedents. One of interest is an American success story—the Tennessee Valley Authority's fight against deforestation in that region's temperate forests. Another is Costa Rica's valiant efforts to save a sizable chunk of its tropical forests. These successes have their critics and caveats, and both could still suffer reverses. But they portray clearly that forests live or die by government policy and that decisions made now about the environment will play out into the distant future.

NEW DEAL FOR THE FOREST

During the Great Depression and the Dust Bowl of the 1930s, much of rural America resembled a developing country, with a growing number of landless people struggling to survive and feed their families. "As bad as conditions were elsewhere in the nation, in most cases they were worse in the Tennessee Valley," according to *A History of the Tennessee Valley Authority*. "The birthrate was one-third above the national average. Levels of literacy were low, and the labor force was largely unskilled. Valley residents suffered from malnutrition; malaria affected up to 30 percent of the population in some areas. More than half the region's three million people lived on farms, and of these, half lived on farms they did not own." The per capita income was $163 dollars—56 percent of the national average.

Much of the region's misery a half century ago was caused or compounded by deforestation set in motion three centuries earlier by the first European settlers. The English, Scots, and Irish who settled the Tennessee Valley found a blanket of rich forests, primarily oak-hickory hardwoods. They stripped the land to make room for homes and farms. Still more trees, writes historian North

Callahan, were used to build flatboats, rafts, and keelboats to carry cotton, corn, whiskey, and other produce to New Orleans via the Tennessee, Ohio, and Mississippi rivers. Beginning about 1890, commercial loggers also arrived on the scene hoping to get rich by tearing down vast tracts of forest.

By the early 1930s, virtually all the Tennessee Valley's virgin forest was gone. While about half the region remained forested, these second- and third-generation stands of trees were severely degraded. The most biologically impoverished areas were frequented by wild fires, disease, and insects. Cattle roamed freely through the forests, compacting soil and trampling any fragile tree seedlings.

Farmers themselves paid the price of this environmental degradation, but they also intensified it by planting such soil-depleting crops as cotton and tobacco on lands already damaged by deforestation. By the mid-1930s, about half the valley's cleared land—much of it on steep mountain slopes—had been abandoned or severely eroded. As the Tennessee Valley's mountain watersheds were deforested, floods and droughts increased and crop yields declined. As a government report written 50 years later put it, "many farms had been reduced to sterile wastelands"—again, a description that fits many deforested developing nations today.

To pull this troubled region out of its slump, the U.S. government in 1933 created the Tennessee Valley Authority (TVA). Still operating today, the organization was one of the most ambitious components of President Franklin Delano Roosevelt's "New Deal" plan to revive the nation's economy. In Roosevelt's heady words, TVA was to be "clothed with the power of government but possessed of the flexibility and initiative of private enterprise." In practical terms, this meant setting up a three-person board, appointed by the president and accountable directly to the president and Congress, to run the organization while sparing it the bureaucracy that encumbered other federal agencies.

TVA's primary goals were to improve navigation on the Tennessee River and to harness the river's power to generate electricity. But TVA had a broader mission, too—managing land, water, and natural resources to bolster the region's economy. Deforestation frustrated all of these goals, so TVA made tree planting and land

DEFORESTATION AND REFORESTATION IN ELEVEN COUNTRIES IN THE 1980s

Country	Extent of Forest and Woodland (in thousands of acres)		Deforestation		Reforestation (in thousands of acres per year)
	Open	Closed	Average Annual Extent (in thousands of acres per year)	Percent per year	
Brazil	392,500	893,700	22,625	1.8	1,403
Canada	430,750	660,250	X	X	1,800
Costa Rica	400	4,095	310	6.9	3
France	3,000	34,688	X	X	128
Gabon (Africa)	188	51,250	38	0.1	X
Indonesia	7,500	284,738	2,300	0.8	410
Mexico	5,250	115,625	1,538	1.3	70
Philippines	X	23,775	358	1.5	158
United States	216,040	523,933	X	X	4,438*
West Germany	545	17,473	X	X	155
Zaire	179,600	1,764,375	925	0.2	3

X = information not available

*Note, though, that the United States still loses more forests each year than it replants.

Source: World Resources Institute (U.N. Food and Agriculture Organization; U.N. Economic Commission for Europe; Country data sources)

restoration a top priority. The fledgling organization set up one tree nursery in Clinton, Tennessee, and another in Muscle Shoals, Alabama, which together could produce up to 50 million seedlings a year. With this new capacity, TVA launched a demonstration program to teach farmers why and how to plant trees on eroded lands. Between 1933 and 1942, some 5 million days of labor went into TVA forestry projects, partly to replant 136,000 seriously eroded and gullied acres.

In 1944, two-fifths of the forest in the Tennessee Valley was in private hands. To preserve trees on these lands and to get new ones planted, TVA had to convince farmers that forests figured into their long-term economic future and not simply as timber to be logged for short-term gain. If that was a hard sell, harder still was persuading large corporations and absentee "treelords" of the need for tree planting and soil conservation at a time when the Valley's unmanaged forests were being rapidly felled to get timber and to open up access to coal, iron, and phosphate.

The fastest way to protect and rejuvenate the off-farm forest would have been simply to get the federal government to buy the land for parks or reserves. But TVA—part private corporation, part government entity—set too much store by private initiative and the profit motive to take this tack, and the agency wanted to stabilize the farmers' future, reclaim eroded lands, and raise valley residents' living standards. So, instead, TVA banned farming on steep slopes and initiated programs in tree planting, soil regeneration, pasture planting, health, education, and rural electrification. Farm forests were planned to provide farmers with income from the production of lumber, railroad ties, veneer, fuelwood, and pulpwood, and TVA stimulated the development of commerce, including the new defense-related industries spawned during World War II, in the valley to provide off-farm employment.

If numbers tell the story, TVA's tree-planting efforts worked. A 1944 International Labour Organization study pegged the number of trees planted by 1942 at more than 150 million, over two-thirds of which helped control erosion. By 1957, some 350,000 acres had been reforested, and in the 1960s, a new program, "Plant Trees—Grow Jobs," inspired Tennessee Valley residents to plant another round. By mid-1980, total forest cover in the Tennessee

Valley exceeded 21 million acres—a million more acres of forest than in 1930.

But bringing the forests back was only part of a larger economic development campaign. While the TVA was revamping forest-management policy, it constructed the dams and reservoirs for which it is now famous and brought cheap electricity to the region. TVA also established an elaborate agricultural demonstration-and-extension program to get the region to adopt fertilizers and new farming practices, and to introduce terracing, contour plowing, and strip cropping to boost production, income, and soil protection. By 1940, corn, wheat, and dairy cattle production had more than tripled on TVA's 15,000 demonstration farms.

Timber and water supplies, erosion control, navigation, electricity, recreation and tourism, and jobs have all been created by federal and TVA policies that support farmers, control waterways, and encourage reforestation, pasture development, and private investments in the region. Watershed conservation has also improved, thanks to policies that have brought erosion and sediment flows under control. But, if this poverty-to-riches story sounds too good to last, perhaps it is. Today TVA is grappling once again with one of the forces that it was created to fight 60 years ago. Ignoring lessons learned by their parents, some landowners in the western valley have begun plowing up cover crops to plant soybeans—a lucrative cash crop—and using other farming techniques that severely erode the soil. Badly damaged, some fields now annually lose as much as 100 tons of topsoil per acre, and TVA is once more launching farmer-education campaigns. And TVA has established large-scale coal-fired power plants that emit sulphur dioxide and nitrous oxides, thus contributing to acid rain that is killing the trees that TVA helped plant!

Taken as a whole, the TVA experience shows how important government policies are to managing and restoring forests and how forest conservation and development can be fundamentally tied to local social and economic activity. Obviously, keeping forests and forest-based economies in good working order entails far more than just planting seedlings.

COSTA RICA'S PRIDE ON THE LINE

Costa Rica is one of the Western Hemisphere's garden spots. And, in the face of at least some of the same economic crises that other developing nations face, its government hopes to keep it that way.

The Spanish colonists who landed in Costa Rica's shores in the sixteenth century named it aptly. This "rich coast" contains an unmatched wealth of plant and animal species: 150 species of reptiles and amphibians, 237 species of mammals, 850 species of birds, and over 12,000 species of plants—all in a country the size of West Virginia. It has more bird species than the United States and Canada combined and twice as many plant species as California, which is 18 times larger. Some experts say that 5 percent of *all* plant and animal species on Earth live in this tiny country—and nowhere else.

With courage and foresight, Costa Rican conservationists, political leaders, and local people have created a system of national parks and protected areas that are in many ways the developing world's envy. Some 3.4 million acres—or 27 percent of its national territory—were under protection in 1990 in 14 national parks, 6 biological reserves, 1 national monument, 1 nature reserve, 12 multiple-use forest reserves, 2 protection zones, and 11 wildlife refuges. Six percent of this protected land is in indigenous reserves. Although most of the forest reserves and parks are regulated, some are still in private hands, awaiting government purchase. But there is much more to the story than these bare facts suggest.

Behind the day-to-day management of these impressive national parks and other protected areas lies a strategy that ties each to the others and to Costa Rica's economic, social, and ecological fabric. Wild nature is to be vigorously protected in "core sites" within larger "regional conservation units" that provide employment for park staff, scientists, and others; water for downstream electricity generation, drinking, and irrigation; erosion control; and tourist attractions, environmental education, and recreation services.

In these 8 regional conservation units, some truly unique socioeconomic experiments are under way. In *Guanacaste* National

Park, *Santa Rosa* National Park, and other protected sites in the northwestern part of the country, for instance, spectacular recreational opportunities in natural forest and beach settings will be preserved, along with the migration routes of animals, including many that pollinate the region's trees or disperse their seeds. At the other end of the country, *La Amistad* National Park forms part of the largest protected complex in Central America (*La Amistad* Biosphere Reserve), comprising a network of 14 contiguous protected areas that encompasses nearly 2 million acres in southeastern Costa Rica and western Panama. Within *La Amistad* Park are several different types of tropical forest, a rich variety of life forms (including such endangered species as the tapir, giant anteater, and all six of the region's tropical cat species), and the headwaters of major rivers that have been harnessed downstream for hydroelectric generation and water supplies. The park also includes lands reserved for native peoples.

If all eight regional conservation units work out as planned, says tropical biologist Daniel Janzen, Costa Rica can retain over 80 percent of its biological diversity. One key is the so-called conservation corridor. A few years ago, Costa Rica's park service bought a strip of forest connecting *Braulio Carrillo* National Park to the Organization for Tropical Studies' (OTS) field station, *La Selva*, which is 21 miles away. For the first time in Central America, a protected area embraces unbroken forest cover that extends from warm low-elevation rain forests to cool mountain "cloud forests" (forests perpetually bathed in mist, created when warm air masses from the Pacific collide with cooler air masses from the Atlantic). Forest fauna can move along this life-giving stretch, up and down slope with the seasons, in search of flowers or fruit, as they do in unperturbed nature. The corridor also gives plants the space to colonize up and down slope, to wetter or drier sites, in response to subtle shifts in the area's climate.

This "corridor" idea has long been touted by conservation biologists and managers but seldom tried. In most tropical regions, as the bulk of the forest is converted to farms and ranches, bisected by roads, and dotted with villages, protected areas end up as virtual islands of forest amid a sea of crops and pastures. Each fragment becomes isolated at a specific elevation and in a specific microclimate and moisture regime. The birds, insects, and other animal species that typically travel up and down slope as the seasons change to find food and exactly the right climate to suit their needs are cut off, and they may face local extinction, as may trees if the animals are seed dispersers or pollinators. The corridor solves this problem and allows agriculture and forestry to coexist.

One reason why conservation works in Costa Rica is that public and private conservation programs and science have entered into a highly practical and mutually beneficial marriage. The Organization for Tropical Studies (OTS), a consortium of 44 U.S. and Costa Rican universities established in 1963 to promote research and education in tropical biology, has supported field conservation since its inception. More than 2,000 U.S. and Latin American scientists have studied at its rain forest field station and at park sites, where many have been gripped by a lifelong passion for studying Costa Rica's plants, animals, and forests.

OTS's impact has spread well beyond the scientific community. Just as people in Detroit talk about cars or people in Hollywood talk about movies, the mere presence of so many biologists in the country has made conservation a common topic of conversation and has generated considerable support for this practical art. Rodrigo Gámez, a policy advisor to former President Oscar Arias and now director of the National Biodiversity Institute, told *BioScience* magazine that his association with OTS "helped open my eyes to the importance of biological diversity." As Costa Ricans came to understand "what all these crazy gringos are doing down here," he added, they came to appreciate their country's great natural wealth more.

Clearly, Costa Ricans largely have themselves to thank for the conservation foothold established in many of their forests. Visiting scholars, international nongovernmental agencies, overseas foundations, aid agencies, and the growing flock of ecotourists have provided scientific support, funding, and moral encouragement. But far more important in this developing country is the conservation commitment that runs through the whole society, from the average citizen on the street to the president. Costa Ricans have established the laws and institutions, come up with the basic funds year in and year out, and produced the legislators, presidents, park managers, and others that it takes to operate on conservation's firing line.

But can Costa Rica keep up its good work in the face of mounting economic problems? Many of the economic scourges of the 1980s plague it, along with other developing countries: unemployment, skewed land distribution, drops in export revenues, and huge foreign debts. Costa Rica's population of 3 million is now growing by 2.6 percent a year—rising once again after a highly effective family planning program curbed growth in the late 1970s. The government is hard-pressed to provide public services to all citizens. In 1987, per capita GNP amounted to $1,610—well ahead of its Central American neighbors but below its own standards of a decade earlier (and less than one-tenth of what the comparable figure is for each U.S. citizen).

As public income falls, budgets for parks and protected areas follow suit. More sobering, even with so much public land committed to conservation purposes and the great strides being made in private nature reserves, Costa Rica has one of the region's highest deforestation rates on lands outside its protected areas. Each year, between 100,000 and 150,000 acres of forest are lost, and, during the same decade that it set aside 1,250,000 acres in parks and protected areas, the country lost 1,842,000 acres of virgin forest. Soon, little harvestable forest will remain outside of the protected areas, and by the century's end lumber will have to be imported. To top it off, the lack of better economic alternatives has prompted many poor Costa Ricans to enter protected forests illegally to prospect and mine for gold—an enterprise that few forest ecosystems can withstand, especially if mercury is used to separate the gold from the crude ore.

Sheldon Annis, in a study for World Resources Institute, attributes Costa Rica's predicament to its large and growing dual debt, the sum of its past borrowing from its own natural resources and from foreign banks. This debt was contracted for good reasons: to boost industry, agriculture, social services for the poor, and the standard of living for all Costa Ricans. But an unwieldy debt is an unwieldy debt, and it has had disastrous consequences.

Writing in *Ethics & International Affairs,* Annis documents the history of Costa Rica's debt crisis. One root cause, he says, was conflicting governmental policies. "Industrial policies that were supposed to have increased exports increased imports instead. Social policies that were to transfer resources to the poor were undercut by economic policies that transferred resources to the rich. Park legislation that was to protect wildlife and forests was undercut by agricultural policies that led to deforestation and landlessness. One set of policies unraveled the benefit of the other."

When the "oil shocks" of the 1970s hit, they drove prices for food and other commodities in Costa Rica upward by as much as 40 percent. Just as the country was trying to shift its production away from coffee, sugar, and the other agricultural mainstays that have fickle prices, the cost of importing raw materials and technology for the new manufacturing enterprises rose. Meanwhile, the demand for Costa Rica's most valuable agricultural exports, especially coffee, dropped. The country was buying dear and selling cheap, with obvious consequences.

Like so many other countries, Costa Rica's government began borrowing heavily from foreign banks, setting itself up for the debt crisis that materialized in the 1980s. Between 1973 and 1982, its external debt grew tenfold, from $296 million to $2.9 billion. By 1986, Costa Rica's debt was $1,445 per capita—second only to Israel's. Because the government had little money to spend on domestic needs, Annis notes, "new land reform efforts became financially unsustainable, the purchase and maintenance of parks was curtailed, roads and watershed basins could not be adequately maintained, scientific research and long-range planning studies became a luxury." Cash crops and cattle provided export income, but the price was paid in higher consumption of forests, land, and water.

Like many other analysts, Annis contends that the very poor "are much harder on the environment because they do not have the minimum assets, the security, and the economic incentive to invest in conserving their physical resources. This is not due to a lack of education, environmental sensitivity, or agronomic skills, but is a matter of practical survival." Necessity drives the poor to cut the forest for subsistence farming, to hunt wildlife, to plant crops on highly erodible slopes and soils, and to dig for gold in the forest. As Annis concludes, "the environmental challenge for Costa Rica in the 1990's is *not* what to do about parks, but rather, what to do about an underemployed, displaced, assetless rural population, that unfortunately tends to consume remaining resources faster as it becomes poorer."

To its credit, Costa Rica has not allowed its commitment to conservation to be scuttled in the throes of economic crisis. Its budget for conservation (and most other activities) has recently fallen, but conservation is still a big part of its economic development plans and programs. By mid-1990, the new administration was laying plans for major reforestation projects and incentives, as much to guarantee the future of agriculture and ecotourism as to give forestry and forest management a boost. Indeed, Costa Rica's incoming environment minister expects tourism to overtake coffee and bananas as the number one source of foreign exchange sometime in the mid-1990s.

One other sign of hope: Costa Rica's debt situation improved dramatically in May 1990 when it and a group of U.S. banks restructured the country's $1.8 billion debt to commercial banks. (This makes Costa Rica one of the first countries to benefit from the so-called Brady Plan, a U.S. offer of new financing to developing countries put forth by Treasury Secretary Nicholas Brady in March 1989.) Under the new accord, Costa Rica will buy 64 percent of its commercial debt at 16 cents on the dollar. If, as expected, the plan saves the Costa Rican government $150 million a year, both economic development and forest conservation should benefit.

Costa Rica's "good news/bad news" story is one of an interplay of forces that are often at odds. Like many other tropical nations, the country is pressed from within by inflation and unemployment and from without by its still sizable debt. But it is richly endowed, and it has shown uncommon foresight in natural resources management, so, if unbridled optimism about its forests seems misplaced, well-grounded hope does not.

TWELVE STEPS TO CONSERVE THE FOREST

As these economic parables from the United States and Costa Rica suggest, such unglamorous concerns as how government programs are focused, development policies formulated, forestry projects planned and implemented, agricultural budgets allocated, and debts managed, as well as what kind of research and information gets sᴘᴏɴsᴏʀed and disseminated, can make a world of difference to a forest and its inhabitants. In particular, 12 steps are needed to keep the forests alive and economically productive.

1. *Redistribute land more fairly.* Government policies that inadvertently promote poverty also invite deforestation. By the same token, where nature's goods and services are fairly shared, people have some incentive to protect forests and use them wisely. Unfortunately, in most tropical countries, the vast bulk of the best tillable land is owned by a small minority of the population, who typically plant high-paying export crops on it. In others, the land is held by the central government and leased for logging, mining, or plantation agriculture. Under either system, the growing number of landless poor will have little choice but to invade the forest unless jobs suddenly open up in industry or other "off-land" occupations.

To keep the forests alive and well, land reform is critical, especially in the Western Hemisphere. In Central America, there is enough farmland already deforested to accommodate today's population and the expected growth through the end of the century *if* it is equitably distributed. With the help of state-of-the-art technology, crop productivity on these lands can be boosted to permit both economic growth and social development. Similar opportunities exist in Brazil.

It requires political courage to take from the rich and give to the poor. But the easy way out must be avoided: giving colonists raw "vacant" lands that, in fact, lie within the territories of indigenous peoples, thus furthering social injustice.

So what's to be done? The first step is squaring land reform with urban development policies: agrarian reform and land distribution cannot answer all employment needs, and new industries must be established in and around urban centers so that the landless don't see conquering the wilderness as their only option. The second is revamping the procedure for determining land ownership. Laws that compel colonists and ranchers to clear land, erect buildings, and plant crops or install cattle in order to obtain title have to go. Their contribution to deforestation, land speculation, and the displacement of traditional forest dwellers is now a matter of public record and shame.

Do precedents exist? Brazil's recent decisions to drop the requirement that tenants must clear land to earn title to it and to establish extractive reserves are moves in the right direction. So is putting large territories in the Colombian Amazon under the control of native groups. More of such programs would provide forest residents and new colonists alike with the social and economic security needed to use the forest without destroying it.

2. *Manage the forests to serve international, national, and local interests.* Forests can be administered at different levels: by central agencies like forest and park services, by provincial authorities, or by local communities. Sometimes the national interest is best served when administration is centralized. For example, in certain forest watersheds, safeguarding stream flow for downriver irrigation, hydropower, or drinking water means making sure that the forest is left unperturbed—clearly not a job for local residents who would have to deny local interests to serve national ones. Similarly, in some cases, it's too much to ask local residents to try to save wildlife sites or species for the good of the global community or future generations when their own jobs and way of life are on the line.

In general, it's the national government's job to watch out for the citizenry as a whole, including those yet unborn, and to cover the country's international obligations, such as protecting transboundary rivers or unique wildlife, and the national interest must figure centrally in the development of hydroelectric facilities, mines, industry, roads, airports, and new towns. But, even if local groups have to make concessions, they should be involved in the planning and decision making and be justly compensated when they sacrifice territory or tradition. For their part, governments that exercise such rights of domain owe it to local communities to spend the money needed to support national parks, forest reserves, agricultural extension, and social services. Too many developing world governments have centralized control over forestlands without backing up this authority with labor, technical services, and the budgets needed to manage the resources and to work closely with local residents.

Where authority and responsibility are out of alignment, one solution is to decentralize control of natural resources. In some federated countries, states or provinces already have control over forests, parks, and wildlife. Other options include regional institutions that work with communities to manage resources. In theory anyway, such "middle management" brings decisions closer to the people affected by them, while protecting the nation's natural resources from excessive claims by minority interests. The emerging state-level forest and park agencies in the Brazilian Amazon are taking this approach, which the Tennessee Valley Authority also uses.

In some cases, even regional management of natural resources is too remote to be effective. Whether in Amazônia, Central Africa, or Indonesia, traditional forest dwellers often know better than any agency or expert how to derive stable livelihoods from the forest without jeopardizing its environmental integrity. As long as population levels and immigration are controlled, local organizations can also maintain nature reserves to serve community interest, as they do in Indonesia.

Traditionally, many local groups maintained "commons," where they farmed the land on long rotational cycles that at any one time left most of the forest standing. But the number of people and interests competing for land make that system unworkable under most circumstances now. Today, land needs to be assigned to ensure its stewardship. The key is figuring out who can provide the best day-to-day management, which, in turn, means determining who cares enough to nurture and protect the forest and all of its bounty and who has an interest in making sure that the forest continues to provide timber, water, wildlife, fruit, nuts, other products, environmental services, and homes to forest dwellers.

Although some national interests will always have to be under national control, experience is showing that it's best to assign responsibility for forests as close to the forest itself as possible. This approach can relieve central government of a tremendous administrative burden, while freeing it to provide important technical services—for instance, demonstrating innovative forest, agricultural, wildlife, and livestock management, as well as health, nutrition, and sanitation practices.

3. *Grant forest concessions as if the future mattered.* In *The Forest for the Trees? Government Polices and the Misuse of Forest Resources,* World Resources Institute economist Robert Repetto shows how the United States and several tropical countries are squandering their forest wealth by making poor bargains with national and international companies—basically, selling timber from public lands at absurdly low prices. With nothing but hefty profits to motivate them, companies naturally remove the best timber as quickly as possible. Indeed, timber operators have little incentive under current law and custom to do anything *except* cut logs without regard for the forest's regenerative future or its potential to provide nontimber goods and services, let alone accommodate the interests and traditions of local people. In the United States, for instance, the forests of the Northwest and Southeast Alaska are harvested under giveaway terms that drain the national treasury and the forest's long-term productivity and value.

How can government policies be overhauled to take both long-term economic concerns and community needs into account? For starters, policymakers need to grant longer-term concessions that give harvesters the economic incentive to slow down and to cut carefully. Before World War II, many tropical timber concessions spanned a century, but by 1987 the typical term had shrunk to from 5 to 10 years—not enough time to give the logging company any financial interest in maintaining the forest. As Repetto notes, 70-year concessions, divided into two cutting cycles, with the second dependent on how the forest is faring, make a lot more sense. Further, governments should renew concessions only if the logging company is managing the forest responsibly.

Governments also need to make the cost of timber-cutting concessions reflect the high price of tropical wood in international markets. Charging more for timber-cutting concessions and making them long-term can force the timber companies to manage the forest properly—reforesting it, protecting it, and maintaining biodiversity, watersheds, and the sheer beauty of its trees. For their part, developing countries will receive a fair return for their timber resources. Between 1979 and 1982, Indonesia received $1.6 billion from its timber-cutting concessions, much of which went to foreign companies. If concessions had been sold at prices set high enough to reflect the monetary value of trees to be cut, that figure would have been $4.4 billion—and Indonesia could have spent some of the added income to improve forest management.

4. *Fortify forestry institutions.* Foresters are supposed to be stewards of the nation's natural resource base and of the supply of timber, fresh water, and other forest-derived commodities and environmental services vital to economic development. Yet, they often supervise *de*forestation to make way for livestock ranching and agriculture. The act of balancing these two paradoxical factors influencing the forest is difficult, and foresters need help.

A changing land ethic only adds to the increasing pressure foresters suffer. Land clearing and timber harvesting at a breakneck pace, whether to make room for rangeland, agriculture, or shelter in the tropics, or to open lands for development or support local forest-based communities here at home, in most cases are simply illogical. Indeed, nations cling to the outmoded cornucopian notion that forest resources are endless and to "cowboy economics" at the peril of their watersheds, timber supplies, reservoirs, climate, and biological diversity. In the 1990s, this old mentality has to give way to a deeper commitment to forestry and to the development of forest management agencies.

A revolution in how we think about and use our forests will come in steps. The first step is for foresters and forestry institutions to work more closely with local governments and communities to sort out conflicting responsibilities. Any compromises they make must be based on respect for the people of the forest and their forest savvy, as well as for the forest itself.

The second step is investment. As owners and managers of forest lands, governments are uniquely positioned to invest in the research, training, and professional development that the field of forestry needs to mature. For many tropical countries, technical and financial assistance from the United Nations and other agencies is available expressly for this purpose. With this kind of support, careers in forestry, especially in tropical countries where they are now typically unappreciated and poorly paid, would no longer be viewed as low-status jobs. Clearly, advancement opportunities, prestige, and pay scales should rise to reflect the importance of this work, both in offices and on the front lines of forest management.

5. *Support protected forest areas and protect more sites.* More than 120 countries have established national parks, wildlife sanctuaries, forest reserves, and other types of protected areas. The 1970s saw a boom in the growth and development of these sites, mainly in developing countries with tropical forests, wetlands, mountains, and coastal and marine environments. But, in the financially troubled and tight-fisted 1980s, conservation agencies watched their budgets shrink and their responsibilities balloon. When the momentum of the 1970s dissolved, the result was a shortage of trained personnel, inattention to management plans, and excessive numbers of tourists, loggers, oil and gold prospectors, and, in some areas, landless people invading forests.

The first step toward regaining that momentum is making sure that areas already under protection aren't receiving it in name only. Most governments have already established more sites than they can care for properly with the funds that they have. While it is certainly better to have areas decreed, even if unmanaged, the vacuum leaves nature at risk and local people uncertain about their future. At least part of the problem is the pathetically low value assigned to natural areas. The real contribution of forests and biodiversity to local, national, and global economies is still poorly understood. Meanwhile, it is tourism dollars, funds from international conservation organizations, and national pride that keep parks alive in many countries. Missing are guaranteed budget, trained personnel and policy support for each protected area, year in and year out.

New forest and wild lands also need to be brought under the umbrella of parks, reserves, or other protected areas. The United States still lacks a national prairie park, for instance, and all continents have important types of ecosystems in need of protection. Fortunately, IUCN's International Commission on National Parks and Protected Areas, The Nature Conservancy, and other groups have already pinpointed these conservation gaps and have prescribed the actions needed to bring important new sites into the "world network of protected areas." So policymakers have been given a head start. The tasks at hand now are to find the funds and to make the necessary managerial arrangements.

Naturally, this work needs to be carefully coordinated with local residents, especially where important sites for nature conservation lie within territories claimed by indigenous peoples. As COICA, the major federation of Indian groups in the Amazon, has declared, the region's native peoples stand ready to work out cooperative arrangements with governments to manage key sites as parks and reserves, even within their territories. This model can be used elsewhere to balance national and local interests and local responsibilities.

6. *Integrate forest and wildlife management with other social and economic goals.* Parks and reserves alone are not enough to protect forests. Even the great national parks like Yellowstone are too small to guarantee that nature will stay wild over the long term. As noted, the vast stretches of land or water that some plant and animal species need to keep extinction at bay may or may not fall within the bounds of a park or a reserve. Then, too, if protected areas are managed as islands—totally independent and separate from surrounding lands where people live, farm, harvest forest, and fish—antagonism builds: elephants stray from parks and tear up gardens; pesticides drift from cultivated fields into natural areas.

To manage and mediate conflicts between nature's needs and civilization's needs, entire regions have to be administered as conservation territories. In practical terms, this means that the public and private institutions that administer agriculture, forestry, conservation, water, and other resources and sectors need to work together.

Precedents exist. Costa Rica's *Guanacaste* conservation region is one. There, local committees representing farmers and ranchers, government bureaus, and conservation agencies are resolving conflicts and reorienting government policies and private perspectives. In the United States, a large tract of wild land in the Adirondacks region of New York has long been managed by state authorities to maximize nature conservation, tourism, and recreation, and to look out for people who have vacation homes or other business interests in the area. Residents have worked with state authorities to protect the forest and waters (though now long-distance air-borne pollution causes problems that can't be resolved within the region). In the Greater Yellowstone ecosystem, representatives of the national park, national forests, wildlife refuges, state lands, farms, and ranches are working out cooperative arrangements for dealing with fire, protecting the grizzly bear, and managing the wide-roaming bison. In Cameroon, people living in the lands surrounding the Korup National Park are (with support from the World Wildlife Fund and other groups) establishing sustainable ways to cultivate wood products, firewood, small farms, and settlements while still giving nature as free a hand as possible.

This approach, often called regional development, is based on zoning. "Transition zones" of one kind or another are created on lands that lie between the wild park and surrounding intensively cultivated lands. In these buffer zones, neighboring people who depend upon the forest can withdraw water, fuelwood, building materials, wild meat, fish, and the like. When wild lands are dotted with small patches of human activity, wildlife habitats can extend far beyond the park itself. The beauty and practical necessity of this approach become apparent if you consider that between 100,000 and several million acres of land generally have to be managed carefully to keep a forest ecosystem from unraveling.

7. *Curb air pollution.* Air pollution used to be a local matter, but it has now become an international and even a global matter, putting Earth's climate and protective ozone layer at risk, along with its forests. Fossil fuel burning accounts for about half of the greenhouse warming that awaits us, as well as most smog and acid rain. As noted earlier, deforestation accounts for nearly one-third of the greenhouse gases, such as carbon dioxide, that humanity releases yearly, and, fittingly, reforestation can help mitigate future climate change. Only a major shift in energy or forest policies, however, can cut to the core of these related atmospheric pollution problems.

Energy sources and patterns of consumption must both change. For the United States, increased energy efficiency is first on the agenda: the booming economies of Japan and some Western European nations are twice as energy-efficient as ours. In other words, for each unit of energy burned, they produce twice as much wealth. Provided that it makes the right fuel choices, an economy using energy this sparingly produces pollutants sparingly and so finds controlling them less of a headache. Shifting from coal and oil to natural gas would greatly reduce the amount of carbon emitted per unit of energy, but only by switching to smokeless fuels (especially solar energy) can we completely eliminate carbon emissions.

Since the global motor vehicle fleet is expected to rise to 1 billion—double today's fleet size—by the year 2010, we simply have to get higher fuel economy and lower emissions from all cars and trucks. Leaner, cleaner vehicles already exist: both Volvo and Toyota have produced prototype family cars that get from 70 to 100 miles per gallon of gasoline, and a Mercedes-Benz hydrogen-powered car developed in Germany and test-driven on Capitol Hill emits no carbon whatsoever.

Other affordable technologies available today can cut the energy needed for electrical motors, home appliances, lighting, and steel manufacture by up to 50 percent. But, unless governments remove hidden subsidies that make fossil fuels look like a better deal than they really are and raise energy taxes to make fuel prices better reflect the true cost of producing and consuming energy (including those of cleaning up pollution), these new technologies don't stand much of a chance anytime soon.

There is good news on the pollution front. Aften ten years of contentious debate, the U.S. Congress passed and the president signed a new Clean Air Act in the fall of 1990. This sweeping legislation takes direct aim at many of the air pollutants most damaging to forests. Under the new legislation, power plants will have to curb their emissions of sulfur dioxide and nitrogen oxides significantly over the next ten years. Total emissions will be fixed or "capped" early in the next century. The Clean Air Act also requires reductions in emissions that produce ground-level ozone—the main ingredient of smog. Other sections of the act address pollution from motor vehicles and emissions of particularly toxic metals and other compounds from our nation's industrial plants.

While it is too soon to judge the success of this legislation, its

tighter controls and new requirements on acid rain and smog will
almost certainly reduce some of the environmental pressure on
U.S. forests. This should not, however, be an argument for com-
placency. In the long run, global warming and stratospheric ozone
depletion may pose graver threats to the world's forests, but most
emissions that contribute to these problems are not addressed in
the new Clean Air Act.

   8. *Promote "debt-for-nature" swaps.* So-called debt-for-nature
swaps are perhaps the most revolutionary new strategy devised
by conservationists to save forests and other ecosystems. Put
simply, here's how they work: conservation groups buy part of a
developing country's foreign debt, which most foreign commercial
banks are glad to sell at a deep discount, having lost hope of
collecting the full amount owed. The groups that buy the debt then
"sell" it to the debtor country's central bank, which translates
the debt into local currency and invests its face value in conservation. If inflation doesn't get totally out of hand, almost everybody
wins.

   First proposed in a 1984 editorial in the *New York Times* by
Thomas Lovejoy, then vice president of World Wildlife Fund-
U.S., the "debt-for-nature" swap concept really took off in 1987.
Bolivia's exchange, financed by Conservation International, freed
up $650,000 of debt to protect 334,000 acres in the Beni Biosphere
Reserve and several adjacent areas. Costa Rica converted $5.4
million in debt at 75 percent of its face value into funds for conservation—a move that prompted commercial banks and The Nature
Conservancy to chip in donations for various park projects. Ecuador converted $10 million in debt into local currency bonds, the
interest from which pays for parks, environmental education, and
other conservation projects and endows Fundación Natura, a key
Ecuadorian nongovernmental environmental organization. The
next year, the U.S. affiliate of World Wildlife Fund began helping
the Philippine government swing a $2-million debt-for-nature swap
that will fund programs in park management, education, training,
and research. By early 1990, ten such swaps had taken place.

   Debt-for-nature swaps are not flawless instruments of social
change. Some critics of the Bolivian prototype say that the prefer-
ences and rights of indigenous forest dwellers have been ignored

and that, in general, such swaps are not equal to the size of debt and environmental problems. Saving tropical forests may be a hopeless endeavor unless something much more comprehensive and fundamental is done to relieve tropical countries' crushing debt burden. But debt-for-nature swaps can help, and debtor-countries' fears that conditions attached to the swaps might impinge on national sovereignty haven't materialized, so interest in this novel form of conservation financing is running high. If the United States and other governments followed the lead of Sweden and the Netherlands, which helped Costa Rica convert $69 million in debts (or nearly 5 percent of the total debt it owes to foreign commercial banks) into $33 million in local currency bonds that support parks, protected areas, institution building, and reforestation, a real dent could be made in both debt and forest conservation.

9. *"Green" the multilateral development banks.* The multilateral development banks have been slow to internalize the axiom that development cannot be economically sound over the long term unless it is ecologically sound. The World Bank, for instance, has often been accused of ignoring the needs of local residents and the environmental aspects of planned development activities.

At last, change may be afoot. New policies at the World Bank call for more attention to be paid to wild lands maintenance and protection when project proposals are reviewed and to working relations with indigenous groups. Further, in May 1990, "the Bank" (as it's called in Washington, D.C.) unveiled its concept for a Global Environment Facility—a new fund that would disburse up to $400 million a year for environmental projects in the developing world. Sustainable use of forests and debt-for-nature swaps in "hotspots" of biodiversity figure on the proposed agenda. If donor and recipient nations agree on the particulars, the facility should be up and running by 1991.

This new approach to borrowing bodes well for environmental projects that promise "returns" only after many years or in places at some distance from the original investment—types of projects that too often have been passed over until now. For the first time, innovative projects to utilize wild plants and animals in rural development schemes, to protect sites where genetic materials of

use in upgrading foods and medicines might be found, and to
manage watersheds to yield water for centuries instead of decades
and to irrigate fields hundreds of miles away may now be "fund-
able" at interest rates that developing nations can afford.

10. *Work with other governments.* The flow of timber and wood
products, like the flow of knowledge, tourists, investment, and
ecological refugees, demonstrates how permeable national borders have become and how great the influence of distant places
and peoples can be. As economic interdependence deepens, so
does the need to establish common policies and laws, exchange
scientific findings and data, and negotiate equitable ways to share
the costs and benefits of enlightened forestry. To achieve these
lofty but increasingly practical aims, governments will need to
break new ground and to strengthen existing organizations and
agreements. Key among these are:

• **The Man and Biosphere Program (MAB).** Started in 1972, this
UNESCO-inspired program sets the stage for cooperation
among governments in science, training, and both monitoring
and managing ecologically important landscapes. "MAB," as
it's called, has set up a global network of biosphere reserves for
keeping representative samples of wild nature alive. In addition,
it tries to make sure that surrounding communities share in
the benefits of such reserves and to carry out research and
monitoring activities to guide management and track long-term
change. Governments can join this program by nominating biosphere reserves to UNESCO and by setting up national coordinating committees to start projects and maintain them once
they have been established. Many forest sites form part of the
network, including the Southern Appalachian area and the
Olympic Peninsula in the United States, the Manu in Peru,
the Selonga and Virunga in Zaire, and the Tanjung Puting in
Indonesia.

The MAB approach has focused researchers' attention on
important problems that tie in with management decisions. It
has also provided a global framework that helps each government see its country's biosphere reserves in relationship to
others. In Mexico and Bolivia, setting up biosphere reserves on

previously unprotected areas has potentially brought long-term security to local people and the forest. Yet, few countries have the funds needed to make the concept work properly and so are forced to simply spread personnel and funds from other parks programs thinner.

- **The World Heritage Convention.** Under this 1972 agreement, governments nominate sites of outstanding natural or cultural value to UNESCO's World Heritage Committee, which calls on outside referees to evaluate the proposals. Sites facing pressing threats from land developers, other invaders, or natural causes are put on the World Heritage "In Danger List." Once on this list, they are eligible for funds and technical assistance from other Convention members. Several key forest sites, typically national parks, are on the list, including Iguaçu in Brazil and Iguaçu in Argentina (border parks), Tai in the Ivory Coast, Sinharaja Forest Reserve in Sri Lanka, and Olympic National Park in the United States. Governments can join the Convention by nominating at least one site on their territory and by joining the international effort to identify and protect globally important spots.

  Uniquely, this international convention is buttressed by a fund administered by the UNESCO Committee. But most of the recognition and funding has gone to the restoration, preservation, and management of cultural sites. Of natural areas, already protected spots—mostly national parks—get most of the attention, and neither UNESCO nor the more than 100 governments that participate in the program has been very eager to identify the sites around the world that ought to be listed, even if these areas have yet to be established as national protected areas or to be nominated for inclusion on the World Heritage "In Danger List."

- **The Tropical Forest Action Plan (TFAP).** Launched in 1985, this global action plan for reforesting watersheds, establishing protected areas, promoting wiser forest management and industrial practices, and combining forestry, agriculture, and livestock management has come under fire for being poorly managed and failing to address local people's needs head on. But, as of 1990, 70 countries were already participating, and several reports on how to get the ambitious plan back on track were being widely discussed by the original sponsors of TFAP—the World Bank, the UN Development Programme, the UN Food and Agriculture Organization, and the World Resources Institute—and nongovernmental organizations, including indigenous groups.

Its shortcomings can't be dismissed, but the plan still has considerable momentum, financial support, and potential going for it. If properly reformed, it remains one of the most important and promising approaches available to address the future of the tropical forest.

- **International Tropical Timber Organization (ITTO).** ITTO was established under the 1983 International Tropical Timbers Agreement, which was negotiated through the United Nations Conference on Trade and Development. ITTO is perhaps the only commodities trade-promotion organization with conservation as an explicit goal. Its semiannual meetings are also a unique forum for producer and consumer countries, as well as for observers from industry and nongovernmental organizations (NGOs). Despite its unique character and potential, ITTO has nevertheless been plagued by a number of problems. Its formal deliberations have often been sidetracked by political and protocol issues, consumer nations have not taken it as seriously as producers, many of its project proposals have been poorly prepared and self-serving, and many members have lagged in paying their dues, leaving its Secretariat strapped for funds. More unsettling, ITTO has yet to demonstrate fully what it means by the "sustainable management of tropical forests" for timber production and how this all-important goal can be accomplished.

- **Biodiversity Conservation Strategy Program.** Since 1989, the World Resources Institute, the International Union for Conservation of Nature and Natural Resources (IUCN), and the United Nations Environment Programme (UNEP) have joined governmental and nongovernmental organizations from around the world to look closely at the root causes of biological diversity losses. The aim is to develop a global strategy and a decade-long action program at the local, national, and international levels to better understand, defend, and use the planet's natural wealth. Far from a "top-down" approach, this program features a partnership with groups from all continents and IUCN's 600 member organizations. Through UNEP, it also has a direct link to the world's governments.

• **The Global Biodiversity Convention.** Many conservationists and governments are lobbying for a broad international agreement that would make governments legally responsible to the international community for conserving nature and natural resources. In 1984, IUCN's 600 members asked its head office to prepare such an international agreement. At the same time, UNEP was directed by its council of member governments to investigate methods of streamlining international cooperation so that major biodiversity issues would get the attention they deserve. The IUCN proposal calls for an international advisory group to list areas that will receive priority international support for their management and protection, and a fund has been proposed to finance this effort. So far, however, there is no consensus among experts and governments about either what types of sites should receive priority or who should contribute to the fund.

11. *Control population growth.* Sharon Camp, vice president of the Population Crisis Committee, believes that world population, which is now 5.3 billion, could stabilize at 9.3 billion by the year 2100 if, over the next decade, governments and international organizations pull together to slow this growth. (For starters, Camp believes that countries should triple their annual spending for family planning programs, which currently total some $3.2 billion.) But most experts now believe that getting population growth to plateau at 9.3 billion is already a lost cause and that the momentum already gathered will take us to between 10 and 14 billion by the early part of the twenty-second century.

Overpopulation has many causes, but poverty and other stresses on the overall quality of life are at least as important as access to birth control. Birthrates will fall significantly, as they have in the United States, Japan, and much of Europe, only if governments make health care, education, employment, natural resources management, access to cropland, fair agricultural prices, *and* family planning services high priorities. In addition, an increase in worldwide spending on family planning aid, policy changes, and priority shifts are necessary. If world population were to reach 14 billion before it stabilized around the year 2120, many natural resources would be under unbearable pressure. But forests would be particularly hard hit: fully 95 percent of future population growth is expected to occur in developing countries, where half the world's forests and an even higher fraction of its species reside.

   12. *Reach a North-South bargain on the forest's future.* If we maintain and use the world's temperate and tropical forests wisely, the main beneficiaries will be the people living in and around these areas, but all of us will benefit also. This basic fact is beginning to sink in. As awareness of the role forests play in our climate and water supplies, and as prospects for finding new foods, medicines, and other products have grown, the issue has engaged both political and moral leaders.

   These leaders, says Gus Speth, president of World Resources Institute, must now sit down and negotiate a new relationship among countries, one that promotes forest regrowth worldwide and the protection and wise use of the forest ecosystem. How would such a "global bargain" take place? First, a tropical country would declare its intent to plant more forests than it cuts, to slow or halt the loss of old-growth trees, to manage forests with the long-term future in mind, and to collaborate internationally to curb pollution, stabilize climate, and protect biodiversity. Then, the tropical country would link up with an industrial country (or two) that would be prepared to make the same commitment and to share the technology, research, expertise, and added funds needed to turn the goals into reality. Next, the tropical and industrial partners would put their many and varied chips on the table. These might include plans to reforest particular areas; regulations governing logging; added development assistance earmarked for sustainable forestry; access to technology for inventorying and planting trees, restoring forests, or harvesting them more carefully; debt-for-nature swaps and other approaches to converting debt into forest conservation; or lowering trade barriers against tropical foods, textiles, and other commodities.

In such a bargaining session, it's easy to imagine tropical partners offering to reforest vast areas, maintain protected areas, or ditch incentives for forest colonization and exploitation in return for debt relief or technical help with inventorying, surveying, monitoring, and analyzing forest resources. The removal of quotas or taxes on tropical fruit or other forest products might also be thrown into the bargain. Tropical countries could also ask northern partners to stop harvesting their old-growth trees and to use fuel more efficiently.

With chips as potentially valuable as these on the table, soul-searching is inevitable. Just how badly do the northern countries want the tropical forest saved? What will they trade to keep greenhouse gases from burning the forests out of the atmosphere? And how serious are the tropical countries about preserving their forest resources and forest cultures, and about stabilizing the climate?

Speth suggests that Japan may be the most appropriate northern partner in the Asia-Pacific region, that Europe should mate with Africa, and that the United States and Canada are the most logical northern partners in the Western Hemisphere. But, regardless of how the partnerships form or whether this type of bargaining or some other is used, governments do possess the leverage needed to bring deforestation under control. Only they can vouchsafe the rights of forest-based peoples and redress the injustices and inequities that have led to the deforestation crisis. Indeed, some local problems simply must be solved internationally.

For this reason, a number of these challenges will surface at the United Nations Conference on Environment and Development to be held in Brazil on the twentieth anniversary of the 1972 Stockholm Conference on the Human Environment.

Whether nations rise to the occasion remains to be seen, but the conference does afford a critical chance to chart a new course toward global cooperation in ecologically sound development. "Let us be in no doubt that this cannot be a conference like any other, one at which more is *said* than *done*," UNEP Executive Director Mostafa Tolba told the General Assembly. "The time to be satisfied with a little, because we believed we could not accomplish everything, is over." Maurice Strong, Secretary-General of the conference, believes that North-South relations could collapse if the North doesn't come up with sizable financial resources for conservation and resource management. Such a breakdown, he says, "could set the world back ten to twenty years from making the changes that are needed—or could even make them impossible."

6

The Forests' Volunteer Protectors

Most of the great environmental struggles
will be either won or lost in the 1990s and
. . . by the next century it will be too late
to act.

THOMAS E. LOVEJOY
Smithsonian Institution

If we care about saving forests, we can't afford to be apathetic in this crucial decade. If governments are sluggish or recalcitrant, citizens have to push them. A critical mass of committed people can overwhelm and reverse official hostility, intransigence, or indifference—witness the United States during the 1960s and 1970s. Civil rights, general opposition to the Vietnam War, women's rights, and environmental protection all spawned mass movements that changed the face of American life.

Eastern Europe is today's most dramatic arena of citizen action. Yet, many people in distant countries are striving to protect forests without making headlines or the evening news. Indeed, some of the most encouraging signs of hope for forests and forest creatures come from private ventures backed by conservation organizations, villagers, indigenous communities, scientists, and businesses.

Working outside of government channels has its advantages. Nongovernmental groups (NGOs) can't make law or sign treaties. But they can represent the rights and interests of people forgotten by the bureaucracy, inject common concerns into the sometimes self-serving political process, spread messages and ideas quickly, and mobilize local support for saving the forests. NGO activity ranges from tree-planting to political lobbying. Indeed, in a 1990 review of recent environmental progress, Linda Starke noted that "the growing number, new roles, and expanding influence of [nonprofit research, advocacy, and support organizations at the local,

135

national, and international levels] is one of the most striking signs
of hope for our common future."

The people, organizations, and projects described here are
merely a sampling of local efforts to maintain the forest. It is
encouraging to witness the ingenuity in hundreds of ideas and the
number of people, estimated at hundreds of thousands, working
to preserve forests at the local level. Still, more good works are
needed if the destruction of the forest is to stop.

SAVE-THE-FOREST ORGANIZATIONS

In the United States, environmental groups range across a broad
spectrum of tactics, style, and focus—from the Audubon Society
to Earth First!—and garner 20 million donations a year. Many
work against deforestation, but some, such as the New York-
based Rainforest Alliance and the San Francisco-based Rainforest
Action Network, focus exclusively on tropical forests. Together,
they are waging public awareness campaigns, raising money to
purchase parklands, and urging governments and the World Bank
to stop funding that contributes to the destruction of tropical
forests. Such organizations have also backed various consumer
boycotts, including one against fast-food chains that are believed
to import Central American beef.

In developing countries, conservation groups are a comparatively new breed, but they are proliferating fast. "Evolving in
social and economic settings unlike those in which U.S. and European conservation groups arose, these nongovernmental organizations are pioneers," writes Lisa Fernandez in the *World Wildlife
Fund Letter*. At home, they must soothe the fears of their governments and their countries' peoples that they are out to stop desperately needed economic growth. Abroad, they have to convince
their counterparts in industrial nations that, without economic
development and some amount of growth, basic human needs
won't be met and conservation will be doomed.

These fledgling organizations are short on time, too. In industrial
nations, conservation groups have had a century of trial and error
to learn the complexities of fund raising, lobbying, and public
education. Indeed, when the student movement of the 1960s rekin-

dled interest in the environment, popular environmentalism found a preexisting base of supporters and political machinery. But, in most developing countries, deforestation and other environmental problems reached crisis proportions *before* the public was equipped to act.

Despite a late start in what may be an all-too-short race to save tropical forests and their species, these groups are beginning to win important victories. Of Brazil's 2,000-odd environmental groups, several were invited to help draft environmental provisions for the nation's new constitution, an action that would have been unthinkable just a few years earlier.

As these grass roots successes multiply, international northern-based conservation groups are learning to share power with their tropical counterparts, in some cases by leaving the decision of how donated funds are spent up to them. The World Wildlife Fund and such U.S.-based groups as Conservation International and The Nature Conservancy also offer local conservation groups training in management, fund raising, and forestry.

Data is another critical commodity that international NGO groups supply. Since 1974, The Nature Conservancy has been conducting State Natural Heritage Inventories in nearly every U.S. state to determine where and how successfully various plant and animal species live—information that officials can use to decide where and how to spend scarce conservation dollars. The impact is startling: U.S. policymakers consult state heritage programs on some 50,000 decisions every year. This approach is now catching on in several Latin American nations in the form of Conservation Data Centers, and requests for help to set up similar centers are coming in from other parts of the world. The World Conservation Monitoring Centre (WCMC), with offices in Cambridge and Kew in the United Kingdom, provides one of the world's most comprehensive data services on protected areas, the status of species, tropical forests, wetlands, economically valuable plants, and trade in endangered species. The popular "red data books" on endangered species and the directories of national parks and coral reefs will soon be joined by much-needed directories of the world's tropical forests.

Turning raw data on the world's forest into useful information is no mean feat. Strapped for time and money, international conservation organizations have learned to set their priorities carefully so they can spend limited funds where they will do the most good. Norman Myers' ten "hotspots" of biodiversity provide one guidepost for such decisions. The logic is compelling: these hotspots account for less than 4 percent of all primary forests but harbor more than a fourth of all tropical forest plants. Another approach, developed by Russell Mittermeier and employed by Conservation International, is to pour heart and soul into the 13 so-called megadiversity countries, where at least 60 percent of the world's plant and animal species are thought to reside: Australia, Brazil, China, Colombia, Ecuador, India, Indonesia, Madagascar, Malaysia, Mexico, Peru, Venezuela, and Zaire.

Conservationists are putting new emphasis on people and the belief that human needs are at least as important as those of plants and animals. In 1985, World Wildlife Fund-U.S. developed a program (now partially funded by the U.S. Agency for International Development) to help improve the quality of life for rural people in 12 developing countries by incorporating natural resource conservation and management into local economic development. In Dominica, for example, a new furniture business based on sustainable forest management is starting up. In Costa Rica, poor farmers are being helped to obtain land titles, develop tree nurseries, and set up a wildlife refuge. In Thailand, farmers are getting agricultural credit to relieve some of the economic pressures that are forcing them to cut trees within national park boundaries. And, in Cameroon, the small-scale harvests of commercially important medicinal plants and the sale of locally produced honey are helping residents of a tropical forest near the Kilum Mountains make a better living by using their forests sustainably.

There may be as many ways to save forests as there are to destroy them. In Belize, a consortium of conservation groups is offering private citizens in industrial countries the chance to "buy" parcels of tropical forest. Anyone with just $50 to spend can permanently endow 1 acre of rich Belizian rain forest. Administered by the Massachusetts Audubon Society, the program has a lofty goal: to create a new preserve by adding 110,000 acres to the 42,000 acres already donated by Coca-Cola Foods. "It's a great gift idea," New Yorker Cathy Travkovski told the *Christian Science Monitor* after her family and friends bought 26 acres of tropical forest in her name for her fiftieth birthday. Travkovski does not really own the land, but she has helped endow it to the people of Belize for conservation purposes. And she now knows this land in a way she never would have otherwise. She has already visited "her" parcel of forest, which harbors such wonders as giant mahogany trees, jaguars, a thousand species of butterflies, and nearly as many species of birds.

VILLAGERS RESCUING FORESTS

Villagers who live near tropical forests and harvest their resources are mounting some of the world's most successful battles against deforestation. What are their approaches? Limited and controlled harvests of forest animals, intense farming of lands already opened so that less forest will have to be cut, fighting for land titles for poor farmers, and, in extreme cases, putting lives on the line to stop the huge development projects that destroy forests.

One of the earliest and most celebrated community forest movements, Chipko, began in India in 1973 when a commercial timber company headed for the Garhwal hills above the village of Gopeshwar. Local men, women, and children ran ahead of the loggers and clung to the trees, preventing the loggers from chopping them down. *Chipko,* which literally means "to hug" or "to cling to," has grown since its first, daring success. Today, members of the movement use similar tactics to protect soils, watersheds, forests, and other ecosystems.

Innovative ventures in animal husbandry also figure into community forestry. On Papua New Guinea's Northern Coast, Roderick Orari is farming birdwing butterflies, which fetch about $100 apiece on international markets. This makes the insects "ounce-for-ounce . . . more valuable than any four-footed livestock anywhere," writes Noel Vietmeyer of the National Research Council in *American Forests*. And you don't have to clear the forest to get butterfly farming going. Quite the contrary, nearby forests are essential because they provide a renewable source of larval insects. Orari, writes Vietmeyer, "is demonstrating an alternative.

. . . Whereas cattle ranching creates an incentive for forest destruction, butterfly ranching creates an incentive for forest protection . . . the trees are the source of the livestock; as they go, so goes the ranch."

In Panama, green iguanas are the latest "livestock." The ranching idea first surfaced in the early 1980s when the *Pro Iquana Verde* foundation noticed that the green iguana, a traditional food throughout much of Latin America, was becoming scarce and expensive because it was overhunted and its habitat destroyed. With the help of Dagmar Werner and other scientists at the Panama-based Smithsonian Tropical Research Institute, Panamanians have been farming green iguanas experimentally for several years with great success. The lizards, which eat natural vegetation and convert this food very efficiently into meat, have thrived in captivity. Their prized meat sells for about $.50 per pound in local markets (roughly $3.25 per lizard). When Panama's political problems forced Werner to move her research to Costa Rica in 1989, she took along 2,350 iguanas reared in captivity, leaving behind several successful Panamanian iguana farms.

Economic and conservation needs are wedded in iguana ranching. "Iguanas now produce meat at about half the cost of feeding other domestic animals," write Judith Gradwohl and Russell Greenberg in *Saving the Tropical Forests*. "Compared to cattle, for example, which also take about three years to raise, iguanas yield the same or even more protein per [acre] . . . [and do not] require any degradation of the land." Indeed, iguana ranching encourages farmers to protect forests and even to plant new trees in the hope of attracting these protein-packed food sources onto their lands.

If lizard husbandry is the lighter side of Latin American forestry, the fight for land for poor farmers is deadly serious. In Costa Rica, a community-based conservation and development organization called *Associacíon de las Nuevas Alquimistas Internacional* (ANAI) is battling this most intractable cause of deforestation. In tropical forests near the country's Caribbean coast, ANAI has established a community-run wildlife refuge and a network of local nurseries specializing in crops that can be grown beneath the forest canopy. The group is also working with local and national authorities to secure land tenure for local farmers so they will have clear incentives to protect land and keep it productive.

In Africa—where social, economic, and environmental problems are legion—many villagers are getting together to defend local natural resources. A new road built near Cameroon's Mount Oku has allowed slash-and-burn cultivators entrance into the area, causing damage that has prompted one nearby village to act. The Mount Oku villagers make their living by harvesting the bark of the *Pygaeum africanum* tree, which contains a substance used to manufacture a drug for controlling urinary problems in men who suffer from enlarged prostate glands. The villagers also keep bees that make honey from the nectar of forest flowers. Afraid of losing their way of life, the community is trying to convince the government to create forest reserves where, like their counterparts in Brazil's extractive reserves, they can continue to harvest nontimber products indefinitely.

Across the continent, some African villages are making great progress against deforestation by planting trees, protecting watersheds, and using natural forests in a sustainable manner. In Kenya, environmentalist and women's rights advocate Wangari Maathai started the Green Belt Movement in 1977 to fight drought, malnutrition, and erosion by planting seedlings on public lands. By 1989, some 50,000 Green Belters, all women, claimed to have planted 10 million trees in 1,000 "belts." In Ghana, the village of Malshegu is managing a sacred burial forest, from which it extracts medicinal plants and other nonwood products, while in Sierra Leone, farmers in Luawa are maintaining the forest canopy to preserve the climatic conditions needed for coffee and cocoa production.

FOREST DWELLERS UNITING

Some indigenous communities are fighting—and sometimes winning—desperate battles against deforestation. Several years ago, when a new road threatened to open up their traditional forest lands to colonists and land speculators, Panama's Kuna Indians created their own wildlife refuge to protect about 150,000 acres of forest. The reserve borders other Panamanian parks, so these protected areas together form one of Central America's largest forest reserves. To keep their part of the park healthy and whole, the Kuna have built visitor centers to help outsiders understand the forest's special ecological features and have hired patrol guards to keep out illegal invaders.

For the Kuna, good organization has paid off. Having already won several battles against the government for land rights, the Kuna knew what to do to halt the proposed road-building project. Today, the Kuna enjoy a considerable political autonomy and have been granted full legal title to their land. The group has also attracted technical and financial support from outsiders, including the Tropical Agricultural Research and Training Center in Costa Rica, the Smithsonian Tropical Research Institute in Panama, the U.S. Agency for International Development, and the World Wildlife Fund-U.S.

Still, the Kuna had to take on some formidable enemies to retain control of the forest, some of whom came from the highest levels of government. In a Worldwatch report, Alan Durning quotes Panama's former president, Omar Torrijos, asking the Kuna: "Why do you Kuna need so much land? You don't do anything with it. . . . If anyone else so much as cuts down a single tree, you shout and scream." The Kuna leader's response illustrates his community's ethic:

If I go to Panama City and stand in front of a pharmacy and, because I need medicine, pick up a rock and break the window, you would take me away and put me in jail. For me, the forest is my pharmacy. If I have sores on my legs, I go to the forest and get the medicine I need to cure them. The forest is also a great refrigerator. It keeps the food I need fresh. . . . So we Kuna need the forest, and we use it and we take much from it. But we can take what we need without having to destroy everything, as your people do.

Unfortunately, the Kuna face the 1990s in difficult financial straits. The flare of worldwide attention—and fickle international funding—have dwindled to a flicker, so now the Kuna are strapped for funds to protect their land.

Far more threatened than the Kuna are the Dayak, indigenous

people who live in Borneo's timber-rich rain forests. For years, Dayak tribes throughout Borneo have given up their lands and traditional way of life as loggers have decimated their forests. Many have had no choice but to work for the logging companies. One Dayak tribe, the Penan, is not giving up. Inhabitants of Sarawak's rain forest, the Penan number among the world's last true hunter-gatherers. They hunt wild game with blowpipes and poisoned darts and harvest fruit from wild palm trees. About 7,000 Penan remain in Sarawak's forests, but their home is falling fast to the logging companies' bulldozers and chain saws. Already, one-third of Sarawak's forests have been logged. Nearly 5 square miles are logged *daily,* and much of the remaining forest is badly damaged. Throughout Sarawak, serious soil erosion and silted rivers attest to careless logging.

Like Brazil's rubber tappers and Panama's Kuna, the Penan want their government to establish forest reserves where traditional life can change at its own pace. In 1987, the Penan began peacefully protesting by setting up human blockades across logging roads, but many were arrested. The struggle came to a head in 1989, when police broke up the largest blockade yet, arresting more than 120 Penan people. Those jailed, many of whom had never been inside a closed room in their lives, spent anguished months in crowded cells awaiting trial.

The Penan's struggle to hold onto their land has at least temporarily attracted international support. Australian filmmakers Jeni Kendell and Paul Tait made a widely distributed movie called *Blowpipes and Bulldozers* that presents the conflicts between Penan culture and the logging industry in Sarawak. Human rights groups and conservation groups have encouraged their hundreds of thousands of members to write to the Malaysian government supporting the Penan's right to live on their traditional lands. Many have staged protests outside the embassies of Malaysia and of Japan, which buys most of Malaysia's timber exports. The Penan even won unexpected support from Australia's longshoremen, who have refused to unload logging ships from Sarawak.

So far, such pressure has only made government officials dig in their heels. One problem is that many of them, including Malaysia's Minister of the Environment James Wong, own valuable logging concessions. Furthermore, though oil revenues are appreciable, they go directly to the coffers of the central government, leaving the states with a strong incentive to augment their own income through timber sales. But, even though the deck is stacked against them, the Penan have vowed to fight on. In a statement sent to Malaysian authorities, 71 Penan people arrested in the 1989 blockade put their case simply: "We love our land and forest, which our forefathers gave to us, very much. We don't want to leave this land."

SCIENTISTS—SAVING THE RIGHT STUFF

A few years ago, researchers who were worried about the fate of species and ecosystems banded together to create a new scientific discipline called "conservation biology." Michael E. Soulé of the University of California at Santa Cruz, a major founder and popularizer of the field, has called it "a crisis discipline" on the model of cancer research. He drew the comparison because both disciplines draw insights from many fields, and their practitioners often must act before all the facts are on the table.

By whatever name, scientists working in this field are among those in the conservation movement's vanguard. They have devised ways to keep and breed highly endangered species in captivity so that these plants and animals can be returned to the wild once politicians and communities agree to protect vital habitats, and they have advised governments on where to designate nature reserves and how to manage them. In one ground-breaking study in the Brazilian Amazon, initiated by the Smithsonian Institution's Thomas Lovejoy, researchers are investigating how large a protected area must be to ensure its species' long-term survival. Knowing the "minimum critical size" needed to keep an ecosystem intact can help managers and planners integrate conservation and development and can help politicians see that conservation doesn't have to be an all-or-nothing proposition.

Some of the most exciting "scientific" victories have been political. In Mexico, for example, scientists at the *Centro de Investigaciones de Quintana Roo* (CIQRO) were the driving force behind the creation of a successful biosphere reserve—Sian Ka'an—in the nation's Yucatan Peninsula in 1986. Today, about 800 people live in the reserve, most of whom make a good living from lobstering. Nearly one-fifth of Sian Ka'an's local residents participate in 20 or so research projects on such locally important topics as spiny lobster biology, coconut palm disease, and techniques for growing basic food crops on small parcels of land.

Conservation scientists in Costa Rica are also working outside the laboratory. The Tropical Agricultural Research and Training Center (CATIE) is helping farmers produce more food on less land, a critical need in this region where rates of forest loss rank among the world's highest. In Cariari, a small town on Costa Rica's Atlantic coast, CATIE researchers convinced beef cattle ranchers to switch to dairy cattle, which need less pasture and provide a more reliable source of income. Part of the attraction was a new system designed at CATIE to compost cattle manure into inexpensive fertilizer. CATIE has also helped create and manage 300 protected areas throughout Central America, and it has trained about 2,000 regional resource specialists over the past decade in wild lands management.

So far, most scientific and conservation efforts have been aimed at saving what's left of our forests and other wild lands. But can degraded forestlands ever be brought back? While some experts remain skeptical, others argue that ecological restoration is a valuable, underutilized conservation tool. Tropical biologist Daniel Janzen of the University of Pennsylvania, for instance, points out that 90 percent of the eastern United States was once deforested, so "we're living right in the middle of a giant restoration project."

Christopher Uhl of Pennsylvania State University is trying to identify all the variables that limit the regrowth of Amazonian rain forests. So far, his work refutes the belief that "the Amazon rain forest has existed in a pristine, cathedral-like state for tens of thousands or even millions of years and that this forest is just now being disturbed for the first time because of the development activities of modern human beings." As Uhl writes in *Biodiversity,* "there is ample reason to believe . . . that disturbance has always been a common feature of Amazon forest ecology." Historically, he asserts, wind has played a major role in blowing over individual trees. Fire has burned the dry fallen materials for millennia. To

Uhl, the recovery of Amazonian forests from such natural disturbances provides hope that they can make another comeback.

Of course, "civilizing" forces in the Amazon today are far more
devastating than natural forces. By any measure, the scale of
disturbance is far larger, and, unlike nature, people don't always
leave disturbed forests alone to recover. On lands cleared for
pasture, cattle trample the topsoil into hardpan, repeated burning
and chemical weeding kill most of the tree seeds that survive the
original clearing, and birds, bats, and other animals critical to
pollination and seed dispersal disappear. And surviving plants
may be too fragile to withstand the heat, drought, and other harsh
conditions that make cleared land so different from their natural
rain forest habitat.

Despite these obstacles, Uhl hopes that he and his U.S. and
Brazilian colleagues can beat the odds and regrow healthy rain
forests. One option is to reintroduce seed-dispersing animals to
degraded lands. If all else fails, the scientists might have to become
modern-day Johnny Appleseeds and deposit the seeds themselves.
Once a few tough, stress-tolerant trees can get a foothold—perhaps helped along in the sapling stage by artificial shade and
irrigation—others might follow. This sort of ecological midwifery
won't solve the Amazonian deforestation crisis, but restoration
efforts will be crucial stopgaps until deforestation can be slowed.

In Central America, easy-to-clear dry forests that once covered
more than 212,350 square miles have now shrunk to less than 2
percent of their original area. But they are making a comeback in
Costa Rica, where Daniel Janzen is spearheading one of the
world's largest restoration projects. The *Guanacaste* National
Park (mentioned in Chapter 5) features 270 square miles of dry
tropical forest fragments and some high mountain moist areas
along the volcanic backbone of the country. These remnants of
what were once huge forests house seeds that, with plenty of
human help, could return the region to its former forested glory.

The first challenge in *Guanacaste* was to stop fires that ravaged
the region during its six-month dry season. Normally, such fires
don't seriously damage large adult trees; here the problem was
that the undergrowth where fragile tree *seedlings* grow was
stripped bare. Under the program, fire lanes were constructed and

round-the-clock fire watches were begun. Some livestock were retained to "cut the *jaragua* grass," a dense pasture grass introduced from Africa that fuels fires and blocks the growth of tree seedlings, and to help disperse plant seeds. A hunting ban now protects the ecosystem's seed dispersers, including such fruit-eating birds as curacaos and guans and such mammals as deer and peccaries.

After just five years, small parts of the *Guanacaste* forest are already on the mend, and researchers expect the canopy to close throughout much of the park within two to five decades. A century from now, the region should be almost free of grass, and in 300 years scientists expect *Guanacaste* to support most of the plant and animal species that the Spaniards found there when they arrived in the sixteenth century.

The success of these restoration efforts depends heavily on knowledge of which plants and animals belong in the natural forest. Worldwide there may be only 1,500 scientists trained to inventory species—far too few to do the job. Yet, as has been clearly demonstrated in *Guanacaste* and in Indonesia's East Kalimantan, this is a perfect job for local young people. A highly trained taxonomist need come in only at the end to identify the species that the "parataxonomists" can't name.

Unfortunately, funding for the scientific work on tropical forestry's front lines has also been skimpy, considering what's at stake. The National Science Foundation estimates that in 1986 and 1987 it spent a little over $20 million a year—about $.08 per American—on research in conservation biology. Michael Soulé and others in the field consider even this paltry sum exaggerated.

Biologist Paul Ehrlich of Stanford University says that conservation biology deserves the kind of money that the United States spends on medical care and research. "If we find a cure for cancer, that may add one or two years to the life expectancy of Americans," Ehrlich told *BioScience* magazine. "But if we don't stop the loss of Earth's species and ecosystems," he added, "we could lose at least 20 years off our average lifespan." In much the same vein, Michael H. Robinson of the National Zoological Park says we need an all-out effort like the one that produced the atomic bomb during the 1940s. In that project, he writes in *Saving the*

Tropical Forests, "a relative handful of scientists, given almost infinite resources and logistic support . . . achieved their objectives in an 'impossible' time span. We need now the equivalent of a Manhattan Project for the future of life on Earth."

In this same spirit of urgency, biologists and other scientists are becoming more politically active. At a 1986 National Forum on Biodiversity sponsored by the Smithsonian Institution and the National Academy of Sciences, nine prominent biologists formed the "Club of Earth," a group that released a widely publicized statement of concern about the species extinction crisis, which members termed "an unprecedented human tragedy." Throughout the five-day meeting, scientists shuttled back and forth between the forum and Capitol Hill, visiting key congressmen and lobbying for new laws to protect forests and biodiversity.

Some scientists contend that getting political is no longer optional. Argues Janzen, the most outspoken of these scientists-turned-activists: "It would not hurt biology one whit if we simply skipped five years of [the work covered in] today's ecology and evolutionary biology journals and put all that energy into conservation of the tropics." Once biologists felt assured that their research sites would be around long enough to study, he adds, "they could gradually work their way back into more esoteric research."

ZOOS AND OTHER WAY STATIONS

While scientists and conservationists do their best to preserve biological diversity in the wild, some remnants of tropical forest species are being saved in captivity by zoos, aquariums, botanical gardens, and seed banks. These few lucky survivors will, like the animals herded onto Noah's ark, get the chance to wait out the storm of global habitat destruction until conditions improve. Scientists may even be able to boost their numbers in captivity. But captive species today will have nowhere to go unless the tide of habitat destruction recedes. If the dove does not return to the ark bearing an olive branch, these unfortunate plants and animals are destined to become, as some scientists put it, "the living dead."

Zoos are a critical last resort, says New York Zoological Society Director William Conway, adding that "when the preservation of ecosystems falters, their fragments may have to be cared for piece by piece." Indeed, zoos could never house even two of everything: worldwide, they now contain roughly 540,000 mammals, birds, reptiles, and amphibians—a total population that Conway points out is about 1 percent the size of America's pet cat population. The space for *all* the animals in *all* the world's zoos, Conway adds, would "fit comfortably within the District of Columbia," a city of about 650,000 people.

In an effort to increase populations of endangered species, zoo scientists have turned to high-tech breeding mechanisms, such as using domestic species as "surrogate mothers" for rare-species embryos or freezing sperm and embryos for reproductive use later. In interspecies embryo transfers, common domestic cows and horses give birth to, and in some cases rear, endangered wild species such as gaurs and zebras. Artificial insemination has been used to breed animals such as Speke's gazelle, gorillas, and giant pandas. But the high cost of high-tech puts it out of reach of developing countries, where most endangered species live. In these nations, limited funds are better spent trying to preserve as much habitat as possible. For this reason, "technology is not a panacea for the disease of extinction," according to Conway. "It is a palliative—a topical treatment with which to buy time." Obviously, the interdependencies among birds, plants, insects, and other forms of life make it virtually impossible to put whole tropical ecosystems on ice.

Yet, zoos have saved some species that were on their way to extinction. They are "rather like a lifeboat operation," notes Ulysses S. Seal, chairman of the IUCN international group of specialists in captive breeding. Over the past few years, Conway says, the world's zoos have bred individuals of more than 19 percent of all living mammal species and more than 9 percent of all bird species. The California condor and possibly the black-footed ferret now exist *only* in zoos, though zoos have also bred at least 18 other species to increase their numbers and have then reintroduced these augmented populations into the wild. Some of these—the Peré David deer, Przewalski horse, red wolf, Arabian oryx, American Bison, Guam kingfisher, and Guam rail—were extinct in the wild until zoos reintroduced them. The peregrine falcon and the alpine ibex, too, have been returned to parts of the world from which they had vanished.

Like zoos, botanical gardens provide a safe haven for plant species whose natural habitats are up for grabs. Most plants are essentially immobile, and many can be kept alive for long stretches of time as seeds, cuttings, or as miniature versions stored in glass test tubes, so botanical gardens don't suffer the zoos' space problems. Plants are also far easier to breed in captivity and less expensive to care for than animals.

But botanical gardens aren't permanent strongholds against extinction either. Conservation outside the natural habitat "is a refuge of last resort," writes Harvard University's Peter Ashton in *Biodiversity*. "The immediate role of botanical gardens . . . lies in research and education rather than in conservation per se." According to Ashton, until recently director of Harvard's Arnold Arboretum, without botanical gardens we would lack essential knowledge about plant populations on extinction's brink and wouldn't be able to manage dwindling species wisely. Yet, such knowledge simply isn't enough. And botanical gardens do not allow plants to continue evolving in response to environmental changes. Instead, they remain frozen in time—a disadvantage when the time comes to reintroduce specimens back to the wild.

Scientists at botanical gardens are now pursuing revolutionary lines of research that overlap with economics, sociology, and other disciplines. Some are tracking down remote indigenous communities to learn which plants Indians use to treat disease. Conservation International's Mark Plotkin, for instance, has scoured the Amazon on trip after trip to learn about and collect medicinal plants used by native peoples there. Closer to home, researchers in industrial countries are pushing for more medical research on such plants, hoping to give developed nations greater reason to spend what's needed to protect these plants' tropical forest habitats. Still others, including Charles Peters of the New York Botanical Garden, travel to remote parts of the world to study plants with commercial value. If the profits look promising, developing countries will leave more tropical forests standing.

All over the world, protected areas, zoos, botanical gardens, and gene banks carefully guard wild animals and plants, including seeds, tissue cultures, and cuttings of the world's major food crops. Conservation is needed both in natural protected areas (so-called *in situ* conservation) and in zoos, gardens, and gene banks (*ex situ*) because the two methods have complementary strengths and weaknesses. Collections in zoos, gardens, and laboratories may disappear overnight during floods, fires, and other natural disasters, technical failures, or social upheavals. And the natural processes that drive evolutionary change pass them by. Collections in parks and other protected areas are, on the other hand, highly vulnerable to pollution, poaching, and invasion by people trying to eke out a living. Only together can these two conservation strategies work.

BREEDING AWARENESS

Zoos, botanical gardens, and museums are more than lifeboats for endangered species. They raise public awareness of the species-extinction crisis. Most of the best zoos today prominently display information about the endangered animals they house. Some, including Washington's National Zoo, New York's Bronx Zoo, Chicago's Brookfield Zoo, Boston's Franklin Park Zoo, and New Orleans' Audubon Zoo, have created special exhibits of the world's most endangered ecosystems, particularly tropical forests.

Longtime leaders in public education, museums are also stepping up efforts to let the public know about the crises of tropical deforestation and species extinction. The Smithsonian Institution's traveling exhibit, "Tropical Rainforests: A Disappearing Treasure," will tour U.S. museums through early 1994. (This widely hailed exhibit followed on the heels of another Smithsonian exhibit, "Diversity Endangered," mounted in 1987 to explain the causes and consequences of species extinction.) Organized with the help of the World Wildlife Fund-U. S., the exhibit features 1 million freeze-dried bats and an imitation fig tree 10 feet tall and 10 feet wide modelled after an actual 70-year-old, 120-foot tree in Panama. Other attractions include films, dioramas, photo murals, back-lit transparencies, video stations, interactive devices, models, ethnographic objects, and scientific specimens.

Exhibit director Judith Gradwohl believes that one way to combat deforestation is to make the public more familiar with rain forests. "The images of jungles in popular culture are not at all the same as what a real jungle is like," she says. Although the exhibit is realistic, she adds, "there will be no biting insects and leeches—this is a luxury tour of the tropics."

As eye-opening as such exhibits are, Michael Robinson, director of Washington's National Zoological Park, has called for a more integrated approach—the "biopark." Combining elements of zoos, museums, and other traditional institutions, the biopark would "create a holistic form of bioexhibitory portraying life in all its interconnectedness." According to Robinson, bioparks will succeed where zoos can't, helping people to acquire a sophisticated understanding of their own place in nature. "Some of the most daunting problems that we face—from environmental destruction to diminishing diversity of species—are centered on the biological effects of modern civilization on all living things," Robinson writes. "If we are to cope with the outstanding problems of the 21st century, the public at large, and decision-makers, in particular, must understand the interconnectedness of the living world."

Robinson is already moving toward transforming Washington's National Zoo into a biopark. A new "holistic exhibit," called "Amazônia," will highlight tropical biology and explore "the problems of reconciling economic development with sustained biodiversity." The exhibit will include plants, land and aquatic animals, and displays showing traditional and current human uses of Amazonian rain forests, along with possible future uses.

Some of Robinson's ideas for bioparks of the future strike skeptics as outlandish. He envisions, for instance, gigantic terrariums where plants and animals can live indefinitely with no input other than sunlight and perhaps even reconstructed *living* specimens of such late great species as mammoths and dodo birds. Robinson admits that some of these ideas are farfetched, but he's not afraid to brainstorm or to go public with notions that raise eyebrows. The only forecast he hopes "fails utterly—one made by a number of environmentalists—is that many of today's species will exist only in zoos or museums a century from now.''

ECOTOURISM ARRIVES

Long considered the arch rival of conservation, business is beginning to jump on the "save the forests" bandwagon. In the aftermath of the Earth Day 1990 media blitz, cynics have said that corporate executives are simply looking for new ways to make a buck or shine up a tarnished public image. But what's important is that both small and large businesses are now making major contributions toward solving the world's deforestation crisis and that businesses have the power, reach, and financial resources to do even more.

Years ago, the travel agents who first dreamed up the idea of "ecotourism" were clearly looking for new markets, not ways to save the world. The idea was simple: offer expeditions to unspoiled, inaccessible parts of the world that natural history buffs will shell out considerable sums of money to visit. Quite by accident, these expeditions carried many economic benefits along with them. Travel agencies needed local guides who knew remote areas well. They needed people to prepare food, drive jeeps, carry packs, and offer overnight lodging. At the most popular ecotourist sites, they needed new hotels. Soon, communities and national governments realized how profitable ecotourism could be. As Larry Tye writes in *The Boston Globe,* "governments and local residents realize that if the forests go, so does tourism, which makes a more compelling case for preservation than sermons by Yankee environmentalists.''

Ecotourism is booming in some parts of the world, and it is spreading rapidly. In 1980, around 60,000 U.S. citizens visited Costa Rica, one of the most popular nature tourism destinations. By 1988, the number had grown to 102,000, a 70 percent increase in just eight years. "Costa Rica has the potential to become the world's leading ecotourism destination," writes Edward Warner in *Environmental Action* magazine. Costa Rica's stable democratic tradition makes visitors feel secure, and within just a few

---

**DO'S AND DONT'S FOR ENVIRONMENTALLY
CONSCIOUS ECOTOURISTS**

"Ecotourism" is a very special kind of travel, according to Karen Ziffer of Conservation International. "It's a mechanism for educating and sensitizing people," she says. Tourists learn firsthand about environmental problems through their planning of the trip and their on-site experiences. She also sees ecotourism as an economic development and conservation activity. "Ecotourism has done much to prove the economic value of conservation," she notes. "Globally, tourists spend several billion dollars a year to see preserved environments." In recent years, nature-related travel has increased 20 to 30 percent, because tourists are afraid the pristine environments they wish to visit will disappear. The biggest challenge for ecotourism, Ziffer stresses, "is to bring the benefit to local people. In many places, too much money leaks out of the local community—to pay tour operators, to import products that appeal to foreign tourists, and to pay for tickets on American-owned airlines."

For those tourists who want to plan an environmentally sound trip, Ziffer suggests that they do the following:

1. *Choose your tour operator carefully.* Ask specific questions to find out if local residents benefit from the tourist trade. For example, does your operator use local guides? Does he or she contribute financially to local conservation efforts? Are you staying in a hotel that is internationally or locally owned?

2. *Educate yourself.* Read up on where you are going and talk to people who have been there. The more you know about your destination, the easier it will be to make ecologically sound decisions about your trip. For example, Ziffer says that for a trip to Nepal she would ask about the kind of fuel to be used. She would seek an operator who planned to use a fuel such as kerosene, rather than wood, since fuelwood use is a major contributor to deforestation in Nepal.

3. *Take a trip sponsored by a conservation organization.* Several wildlife groups offer vacations or study trips to tropical

(continued)

```
┌────────────────────────────────────────────────────────┐
│         DO'S AND DONT'S FOR ENVIRONMENTALLY             │
│         CONSCIOUS ECOTOURISTS      (continued)          │
├────────────────────────────────────────────────────────┤
```

locations. (See the listing at the end of the book in Appendix 1 for the names of some of these organizations.) The revenue from these trips helps fund the conservation efforts of the organizations and provide jobs for the community and funds for local conservation activities.

  4. *Be a responsible traveler.* When you are on your trip, be careful about how you interact with the environment. For example, says Ziffer, if a guide asks you to stay on a trail, do so. Most such guidelines are set to help preserve the natural surroundings for generations of tourists.

days an energetic ecotourist can visit lowland rain forests, high-elevation cloud forests, dry forests, active volcanoes, rushing river rapids, and remote, palm-lined beaches. Tourism and parks already bring in more foreign currency than anything except coffee and bananas, and Costa Rica's new environment minister expects nature tourism to become the number one money-maker by the mid-1990s.

Another popular ecotourism spot is Rwanda, where tourists flock to see the mountain gorillas made famous a few years ago in *Gorillas in the Mist*, a book, and later a movie, about gorilla researcher Dian Fossey, who was murdered in December 1985. Visitors to the country's *Parc Nacional des Volcans* pay $170 each to view the gorillas for an hour. Rwanda's government uses the money to protect the forest and prevent poaching. Today, Rwanda's second-largest source of foreign currency is eco-tourism.

But ecotourism also has its dark side. In some cases, much of the tourist dollar goes into foreign rather than local pockets. If local residents are hired only for menial, low-paying jobs while foreign travel agencies make off with bountiful profits, tourism takes on a colonialist hue and generates resentment rather than support for national parks and forests.

Then, too, sometimes ecotourists step up pressure on parks and reserves, rather than reducing it. In Nepal, the number of travel lodges for foreign trekkers grew from 1 or 2 in 1970 to about 50 in 1987. To heat these new lodges, their owners turned to nearby forests for fuelwood, accelerating deforestation in the region and even in some protected areas that the tourists came to visit. Tourism has also driven up the cost of living in Nepal, forcing some locals pressed for cash to exploit forests. But, since a 1987 tree census showed just how far deforestation had gone, lodge owners have agreed to heat with kerosene instead of wood. And, to boost the area's standard of living, a Nepalese conservation group was established to collect fees from foreign tour operators; so far, these fees have paid for a school, the region's first clinic, and nurseries of young trees that can be planted in the wild or harvested for food.

Another problem is that ecotourism can be simply too much of a good thing. As ecotourism's popularity grows, hordes of visitors may disrupt forests and other habitats, even if they don't directly contribute to deforestation, as they have in Nepal. In the worst case, some species could be lost. But Daniel Janzen, who expects much of the support for *Guanacaste* National Park to come from tourist as well as research dollars, thinks this threat is exaggerated. If tourists trample a small patch of a tropical forest, he says, it's a small price to pay to permanently preserve the rest. "I will pay 5 percent of any tropical national park's biodiversity to ensure the survival of the other 95 percent," Janzen says.

Of course, there are ways to minimize tourism's ecological damage. Ecuador's Galapagós Islands, a tourist draw for decades, stand as one example. The islands' unique character and species survive because tourism is carefully regulated, and the birdwatchers, island hoppers, and others who make the trip play by the rules. Visitors stay on the trails, eat, sleep and leave their waste on tour boats or in the few residence hotels. They also pay a hefty fee, most of which is ploughed directly back into the islands' community development and the national park.

Some ecotourism operators go far beyond simply controlling potential damage. Giovanna Holbrook of Holbrook Travel in Gainesville, Florida, learned in 1986 that 500 acres of Costa Rican rain forest were about to be logged. Putting up her home as equity to borrow $520,000 from the bank, she bought the land and turned it into a private nature reserve where she now sends her nature-loving clients. She also hired local people, some of whom would have worked on the foiled logging operation, to build and run the reserve's lodge. "We must provide an income to these people and not break the environment," Holbrook told *Environmental Action*. Various ecotourism companies also give some of their profits to host countries and encourage clients to contribute funds, too.

THE GREENING OF BUSINESS

Utility companies, never before among the environmental vanguard, are the newest troops in the war on deforestation. One electrical company executive who is also an environmentalist is Roger Sant, chairman of Applied Energy Services (AES) in Arlington, Virginia. In 1989, AES, which was then building a coal-fired power plant in Connecticut, wanted to find a way to offset the 15 million tons of carbon the plant would release during its expected 40-year lifetime. Basing its decision on an analysis performed by World Resources Institute (WRI), the company funded a CARE reforestation project in Guatemala, 2,000 miles away from its power plant. With additional support from the likes of CARE, WRI, the Guatemalan government, U.S. AID, and the Peace Corps, AES expects this "carbon offset project," hailed by *National Geographic* as "the most sensible and imaginative program yet conceived to put the industrial world's money where its mouth is," to help save Guatemalan forests. By providing poor farmers with alternative sources of lumber, firewood, and fodder, AES plans eventually to offset emissions from all its power plants with tree-planting projects. Already a dozen other utility companies have asked for help starting such programs; if this one succeeds, trees-for-carbon-dioxide swaps could have a promising future!

A major U.S. trade association has also shifted gear in response to the deforestation crisis. The American Forestry Association (AFA), which once catered almost exclusively to commercial interests, today embraces a broader mission. In 1989, it launched a nationwide public-awareness campaign, Global Releaf, to get Americans to plant 100 million trees in their communities by 1992. If successful, AFA officials say, the campaign will help offset U.S. emissions of carbon dioxide. One hundred million young, growing trees can absorb considerable amounts of carbon dioxide; strategically placed, the mature trees will also provide enough shade to reduce demand for air conditioning. All told, AFA's program could absorb enough carbon dioxide and provide enough natural air conditioning to reduce the U.S. carbon output by almost 10 million tons a year, while saving the American consumer $2 billion in annual energy costs. Even if, as some scientists contend, these claims pale beside the magnitude of global carbon dioxide emissions, a valuable first step is being taken and the campaign's educational value is incontestable.

Some ecological entrepreneurs are simply trying to come up with new products and sales gimmicks. Peter Max, for instance, sells his "Save the Rain Forest" T-shirts for $45 apiece. What percentage of the proceeds have been donated to groups working to save rain forests? "Up to this point [we've] only been able to devote Peter's posters and his time," Max's public relations director told *Newsweek* magazine, which added: "In other words, not a penny so far."

But the interests of entrepreneurs can overlap with those of conservationists. Ben & Jerry's Homemade Ice Cream, Inc., for example, has come up with new flavors, such as Rainforest Crunch, that feature Brazil nuts, cashews, and exotic fruits such as *assaí* and *cupuaçu* that grow only in tropical rain forests. While Ben & Jerry's certainly wants to beat out its competitors by offering more unusual ice cream, the company says it also wants to create markets for tropical products harvested from intact rain forests.

Ben & Jerry's has plenty of company among businesses trying to do good while doing well. A British cosmetics chain, The Body Shop, is buying Amazonian herbs to produce a new line of rain forest cosmetics. Florists are promoting wreaths made from *xate* palm, derived from *chamadorea* plants that grow in Guatemalan rain forests. Some manufacturers are even promoting condoms made of Amazonian rubber. According to The *Boston Globe,* they

*"It's great! You just tell him how much pollution your
company is responsible for and he tells you how many
trees you have to plant to atone for it."*

plan to promote these products with the slogan "Defend yourself,
defend the forest."

Jason Clay of Cultural Survival in Cambridge, Massachusetts,
is one of the leading promoters of using the profit motive to save
tropical forests. "We want to show that a living rain forest makes
more money than a dead rain forest," he told *Newsweek*. On a
recent trip to Brazil, Clay collected 1,500 pounds of fruits, nuts,
palms, and other forest goods that he believes could be turned
into marketable products. But there's a catch to his approach.
Some products that can be sustainably harvested from forests,

including rubber and fruits such as mango and passion fruit, can also come from plantations that have supplanted forests, and consumers would not be able to tell the difference. Clay thinks the way around this problem is to mark products with a stamp or a seal, indicating that they have been taken from forests without harming them.

Friends of the Earth-U.K. has already come up with a way to let British consumers know which tropical timber products to buy. It awards a Seal of Approval to companies—loggers, retailers, manufacturers, importers, shippers, and architects—that use only tropical timber obtained in an ecologically sound way. Companies can display the seal in shop windows, advertisements, and on products. Several firms have already qualified for the Seal of Approval, says the organization, and the idea seems to be catching on. This general approach, often called "green consumerism," is used widely in Europe to let consumers know if products are biodegradable, recyclable, or otherwise environmentally benign and is getting off the ground in the United States with the formation in early 1990 of Green Seal, Inc.

Each of these projects tackles only a small piece of an enormous problem. For example, if tree planting were used to offset all the carbon dioxide generated by fossil fuel burning, a whole continent of trees would be necessary—and carbon dioxide is only half the greenhouse problem. And, unfortunately, no matter how many seedlings we plant, species loss will be rife. New stands of trees can't for centuries, if ever, match the complexity and wealth of the forest primeval. So planting trees can't "solve" either global warming or the loss of biological diversity. But it can mitigate both, and it's only one effort among many. The lack of a complete solution to intertwined global problems doesn't argue for abandoning partial fixes but, rather, for multiplying them enough to make this decade count.

7

What Can You Do?

Human history becomes more and more a
race between education and catastrophe.

H. G. WELLS

Modern science has breathed new life into the ancient idea of
Earth as a living organism, an idea with which even intellectuals
were comfortable until the nineteenth-century explosion of knowledge fractured science into a host of separate disciplines. James
E. Lovelock, the British biochemist and medical expert who in
1972 proposed that we are "standing on a superorganism rather
than just a ball of rock," named the theory "Gaia" after the Earth
goddess of the ancient Greeks. According to Lovelock, the Gaia
theory "affects even Darwin's great vision, for it may no longer
be sufficient to say that organisms that leave the most progeny
will succeed. It will be necessary to add the proviso that they can
do so only so long as they do not adversely affect the environment."

It has taken us a long time to learn just how adversely we are
affecting the environment, partly because scientists have only
recently realized the extent to which nature itself is ever-changing.
In this planetary experiment that our species is running, it can be
hard to sort out our own influence on the environment from that
of forces beyond our knowledge and control. But, while experts
wrestle with other uncertainties, our motto has to be "go easy."
It's one thing if the world that now suits us so well slowly evolves
out of human beings' "comfort zone." It's quite another if we
blindly make it happen ourselves.

Predictions of the forests' future may err in either direction,
but doesn't caution make sense? If in the next century the worst

161

prognostications turn out to have been too gloomy, our children and theirs will reap the windfall. By the same token, if we cling to rosy assumptions that turn out to be false, our children and theirs will be forced to pay our outsized debts. Unlike pollution, toxic wastes, watershed destruction, and even soil loss—all of which can be put right in a matter of generations or centuries—species extinction is forever. Although new species would evolve over millennia, the 25 percent or more of Earth's species that we stand to lose in the next quarter century will not be restored. By now it's clear that tropical forests should be protected because they are both home and livelihood to millions of people and because they will be the source of medical advances and future foods, as well as a hedge against climate change. But an overarching moral case can also be made: very simply, it would be wrong to destroy these millions of fellow travelers on our planet. Diminishing this wealth of species is, according to Harvard biologist E. O. Wilson, "the folly that our descendants are least likely to forgive us."

Previous chapters have pointed out what governments can do and what local groups, businesses, and conservation organizations are doing to save forests. But what can individual Americans do, given the global scope of the problem? Each of us *does* make a difference. The sum of our actions makes the United States a force in the world, for good or ill. And every day our choices make each of us part of the problem or part of the solution. While our numbers may be comparatively few and our population growth rate low, the impact of each American is far greater than that of most other citizens around the world because our per capita demands for minerals and natural resources are so extraordinarily high.

Conserving forests at home and abroad is a complex task. There are forests that need help in many countries, each with its own peculiar set of problems and challenges. How can the individual make a difference? How can you focus your limited time and money on the items of greatest interest to you? Here are a few suggestions. For details on how to pursue them, consult the appendices for suggested readings and names and addresses of conservation organizations, national and international aid organizations, and U.S. government contacts.

WHAT YOU CAN DO

• **Educate yourself.** First of all, learn all you can about tropical deforestation and about the condition of forests in the United States and in your own region. For starters, try to acquire an understanding of the difficult social and economic problems tropical nations face and of the kinds of help the United States and other industrial nations should be offering them. Also find out what must be done in the United States to save our own forests. Gather information about the various perspectives in the Pacific Northwest debates over old-growth forests. Wrestle with the issue of how jobs in forest-based communities can be saved or shifted as we move to protect the few remaining stand of old trees and with the issue of how the forestry schools in those regions can spark leadership and fresh thinking.

How secure is the forest in your own neighborhood? Can it be bulldozed overnight for another shopping plaza? Do your local zoning regulations provide sufficient protection? Do they even consider the forest as a category of land use to be protected and managed in a special manner? Find out.

If you answer these questions for yourself, you should end up with a list of topics and places that you think deserve your attention, some of your time and commitment, and a bit of personal cash. The challenge is huge, and you will have to choose your shots carefully.

• **Spread the word.** Armed with this information and intelligence, get your family, friends, and neighbors involved. Mealtime conversation about the plight of the forest, forest peoples, and plants and animals is a good place to begin. Also, encourage kids to prepare their term papers and class projects about forest issues. If you are an extrovert, organize lectures, movies, slide shows, poster exhibits, and study groups in museums, libraries, places of worship, and shopping centers. Encourage your local schools to build conservation of forests and biological diversity into their science curricula. Suggest that school groups and neighbors take advantage of the traveling Smithsonian Institution exhibits on biodiversity and tropical forests. Take advantage of the excellent booklets, journals, and newsletters produced by conservation groups that can help you in passing the word.

• **Vote.** Find out how local, state, and national candidates for office stand on the issues you and your family and friends have identified as important. Give your time, money, and vote to those candidates who have the greatest commitment to conserving forests and their ecosystems. According to a recent Gallup poll, 76 percent of Americans consider themselves environmentalists; yet, nearly half the electorate sat out the 1988 election. If we as voters come to understand what preserving the earth demands—of us and of government, business, agriculture, and industry—we can form an environmental bloc that can push the country toward needed policy changes. Work particularly closely with local elected officials—the town, zoning commission, and county and state officeholders. After all, they make decisions that will directly affect you.

• **Send a message to Washington, D.C.** Take a panoramic view of deforestation, too. Write to the president and your members of Congress and ask what they are doing nationally and internationally to stop deforestation. Request information on what bills they are drafting and promoting on forest issues. Urge them and other government officials to preserve our forests in Alaska, Hawaii, Puerto Rico, and the Pacific territories. Insist that the United States pay its fair share of expenses for the international agreements and conventions that help conserve forests and wildlife. Let them know that you want national energy and transportation policies that will put an end to automotive and industrial pollution—a major cause of forest loss in the United States and Europe. Several nongovernmental organizations specialize in these legislative and policy aspects of forest conservation, and the newsletters they provide to their members will keep you up-to-date on forestry developments and suggest plenty of further opportunities for action.

• **Write more letters.** Also write—on recycled paper, of course—the World Bank, the Inter-American Development Bank, the U.S. Agency for International Development, and the various private organizations that sponsor development projects in the tropics. Ask them for information on the projects they are sponsoring, and encourage them to fund only sustainable, nondestructive uses of tropical forests. You may wish to focus particularly on Amazônia, Indonesia, Zaire, and other biologically rich tropical places. In this way, you can track progress and relate it to your own reading and to television specials on these areas.

Don't forget the positive side of life. Some very important steps toward saving forests are being taken on Capitol Hill, at the World Bank, and within the U.S. Agency for International Development and other government agencies and institutions. So don't hesitate to write to *commend* persons or organizations that have seen the light and have taken enlightened action to prove it.

• **Join conservation organizations.** You should consider joining one or several conservation and environmental groups that represent your interests and that can help keep you informed and involved. Pick groups that give you contact at the local, national, and international levels. Most specialize in particular roles, topics, and regions, whether they are legislation or policy issues, wilderness, hunting and fishing, national parks, wildlife and species preservation, or indigenous affairs. Many work on a family of issues that includes environmental, population, health, and economic development concerns. No doubt you can find one that matches your interests and point of view.

• **Donate time and money.** Some of these groups provide funds and technical assistance to governmental agencies and nongovernmental groups working in tropical countries to improve forest and park management and rural development. You may wish to support field action projects with your donations. No contribution is too small. If you'd like your donation to go to a specific project or country, ask for an organization's annual report and earmark your contribution for a project that looks particularly good. You can also donate money directly to grass roots organizations working in your neighborhood or in the tropics. A country's embassy or an international NGO that works directly with grass roots organizations can help you find out more about them.

- **Visit tropical nations.** Your tourist dollars will contribute to these nations' economies while enlarging your understanding of tropical countries and their people. Visit national parks and see what a tropical forest is really like, especially in countries where you have special interest. Stay in locally owned hotels instead of international chains so that tourist income will go to the local community. If you travel with a tour group, pick one that donates some of its profits to conservation. Consider taking a study tour to really deepen your knowledge of forests. When you return home, write to the country's government, letting officials know how much you enjoyed their parks and other natural scenery. For detailed information on ecotourism, consult the summer 1989 issue of the magazine *Buzzworm* (*Buzzworm* back issues are available from 188 16th Street, Boulder, Colorado 80302; 303-442-1363) or one of the new books on ecotourism.

- **Clean up your own act.** Once you have a clear fix on the deforestation crisis, you will want to bring your own life style in line with what you espouse for the rest of the world. We are a nation with a consumption problem. So, to begin with, recycle your newspapers and other trash. Contact your local Department of Public Works to find out where the nearest recycling centers are. Cut back on your use of paper, fuel, and other materials that use natural resources.

- **Invest wisely.** Several investment groups have instituted funds of stocks and bonds that are environmentally benign for those of us who don't want to sink our hard-earned savings into polluting industries and other unacceptable activities. Ask a broker for details on where the money goes and specifically for investment options that are consistent with forest protection and other environmental concerns.

REUSING RESOURCES

TABLE 1. RECYCLING IN SELECTED COUNTRIES

Country	Annual Paper Consumption (pounds per person)	Annual Recycling Rate (in percentages)
Brazil	64	29
Hungary	132	37
Japan	326	45
Nigeria	7	2
Spain	156	40
Sweden	477	34
United States	580	26
West Germany	346	35
Estimated world average	80	24

Source: Earth Care Paper Company

TABLE 2. RECOVERY RATE FOR ALUMINUM, PAPER, AND GLASS IN SELECTED COUNTRIES, 1985 (PERCENTAGES)

Country	Aluminum	Paper	Glass
Netherlands	40	46	53
Italy	36	30 (1983)	25
West German	34	40	39
Japan	32	51 (1983)	17 (1984)
United States	28	27	10
France	25	34	26
United Kingdom	23	29	12
Austria	22	44	38
Switzerland	21	43	46
Sweden	18	42	20

Source: Pollock, Cynthia. *Mining Urban Wastes: The Potential For Recycling* (Washington, D.C.: Worldwatch Institute, 1987).

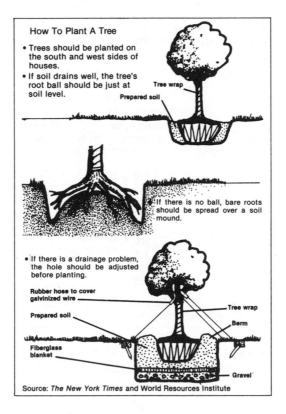

How To Plant A Tree

• Trees should be planted on the south and west sides of houses.
• If soil drains well, the tree's root ball should be just at soil level.

Tree wrap
Prepared soil

If there is no ball, bare roots should be spread over a soil mound.

• If there is a drainage problem, the hole should be adjusted before planting.

Rubber hose to cover galvinized wire
Prepared soil
Tree wrap
Berm
Fiberglass blanket
Gravel

Source: *The New York Times* and World Resources Institute

• **Act locally.** Finally, no matter where you live, you can do something in your area—your own backyard. If you live in Hawaii, Alaska, or the Pacific Northwest, get involved in campaigns to protect your local tropical or old-growth forests. If you live in New England, California, the Appalachian mountain region, or other areas where trees are dying from air pollution, join local groups fighting to halt dangerous emissions. Find out whether your community is participating in the American Forestry Association's Global Releaf program. Consider starting a tree-planting project of your own. At a minimum, plant a tree.

WHY US?

For several reasons, this book has been directed squarely at U.S. citizens. We number among the major users of products made from tropical trees, and some of our own rain forests are imperiled and embattled. What's even more important is that our government and foreign-assistance policies can help make or break tropical forests in the next decade or two. If enough of us make a commitment that's real—not just a bow to "rain forest chic"—and get educated, agitated, and involved, we can make a critical difference.

EPILOGUE

Last Stand for North America's Old-Growth Forests

What we are doing to the forests of the world is but a mirror reflection of what we are doing to ourselves and to one another. As Gandhi said, "An eye for an eye only makes the whole world blind."

CHRIS MASER
Forest Primeval

The Pacific forest is a triumph of life over adversity.

CATHERINE CAUFIELD
"The Ancient Forest"

If a tree falls in the forest and nobody hears it, does it make a sound? This question—a perennial favorite among freshman philosophy students—reminds us of why it's difficult to drum up support for saving tropical forests. If you live thousands of miles from the nearest tropical forest, working to save it becomes at least partly a matter of faith.

With North America's last vestiges of primeval forest, the story is different. For millions of Californians, Oregonians, Washingtonians, and Alaskans, these old-growth forests are a source of income, inspiration, pride, and, quite recently, conflict. For millions more who simply visit or read about these now embattled forests, they are a touchstone of the wilderness and the stopping place of two centuries of westward expansion that transformed everything in its path. And, to the rest of the world, the fate of these breathtakingly beautiful and ecologically vital forests is a litmus test of Americans' commitment to keeping the world's great forests alive.

While more of the United States is forested today than at the

170

turn of the century, most of this forest outside of the national parks and other reserves is secondary forest—stands that have regenerated naturally or have been replanted. The "virgin timberlands that once covered much of the country have shrunk to a prized strip in the Far West," writes Timothy Egan in the *New York Times*. These remnants of ancient forests outside our parks and wilderness areas are rapidly disappearing today, the toll of commercial logging. Already, 80 percent of the 19 million acres of old-growth forest that once blanketed the region have been harvested.

Old-growth forests are worth the fuss that conservationists make over them. Acre for acre, these stands contain well over twice as many tons of organic matter as the lushest tropical forests. These ancient trees "grow vaster than empires, and more slow," to use Andrew Marvell's line. Some that were saplings when the Normans invaded Britain in 1066 are now 300 feet tall and 50 feet around—and still adding a new growth ring every year. As Catherine Caufield wrote in *The New Yorker* in May 1990, "If human beings were as efficient in supporting themselves as these forests are, one square mile would be enough land to sustain nearly three million people." The standing dead trees (called "snags"), hollow tree cavities, ferns, mosses, and other forms of rich organic matter that contribute to this tremendous mass also make this type of forest hospitable to plants and animals that can survive nowhere else. And a wide range of tree ages and sizes can be found in long-lived forests: growth is definitely not at a standstill.

The Pacific old-growth forests extend for about 2,000 miles in a narrow band along the western side of the Cascade Mountains of Oregon, Washington, and California, through Canada and into Alaska's panhandle. Who owns them is no mystery; it's the federal government. But how much is left of these forests is hotly disputed. A few years ago, the U.S. Forest Service estimated that 6 million acres of these vestigial ancient forests still stand on state and federal public lands in the Pacific Northwest and 9 million acres in Alaska. Independent scientists peg the acreage far lower. In 1988, forest ecologist Peter H. Morrison concluded that in 6 of the 12 national forests in the Pacific Northwest, 1.1 million acres of old-growth forest remain—a far cry from the 2.5 million acres

---

THE DOUGLAS FIR: PORTRAIT OF AN
OLD-GROWTH TREE

AGE: 400 to 1,000 years old
SIZE: 300 feet tall, 50 feet around
NATURAL RANGE: Throughout Rocky Mountains, from Pacific Northwest and northern California to western Texas.
NUMBER OF NEEDLES: 60–70 million
LENGTH OF NEEDLES: $\frac{1}{2}$ to $1\frac{1}{2}$ inches
AGE AT WHICH TREE PRODUCES CONES: 12 years
SIZE OF CONES: $1\frac{1}{2}$ to $4\frac{1}{2}$ inches
SPECIES LIVING ON TREE: According to Catherine Caufield, "at least forty-five vertebrate species, from the northern flying squirrel to the rare and beautiful northern spotted owl, will nest or feed only in the cavities of old-growth trees."
SPECIES DEPENDENT ON TREE: tailed frog, Pacific giant salamander, mice, 168 other mammals, birds, reptiles, and amphibians, and countless species of lichen, moss, and insects
COMMERCIALLY VALUABLE PRODUCTS HARVESTED FROM TREE: truffles (the fruit of underground fungi) and enough timber to build an average single-family house
AMOUNT OF CARBON IT KEEPS OUT OF THE ATMOSPHERE: 400 tons over its lifetime
Sources: Catherine Caufield, "The Ancient Forest," *The New Yorker,* May 14, 1990; G. H. Collingwood et al., *Knowing Your Trees.* Washington, D.C.: American Forestry Association, 1974; David Kelly and Gary Braasch, *Secrets of the Old Growth Forest.* Salt Lake City: Gibbs Smith, 1988; and World Resources Institute.

---

the Forest Service claims those 6 forests contain. After the Wilderness Society published Morrison's study, the Forest Service revised its estimates downward, but they are still generally higher than Morrison's.

Whatever the true tally, logging is fast and furious on old-growth forestlands today. A record 5.5 billion board feet were logged from 19 national forests in the Northwest in 1988, about 20 percent more than a decade ago. Most of this timber came from the biggest trees, which were at least two centuries old. According to the Wilderness Society, in 1987 "the timber industry was logging an estimated 170 acres of old growth—the equivalent of 129 football fields—every day."

Much of the pressure to log our last ancient forests has come from outside our borders. Foreign timber companies, mainly Japanese, are outbidding U.S. companies for logs taken from state and private lands. According to Timothy Egan, one of every four logs cut from the West Coast, including Alaska, is shipped overseas. Representative Peter DeFazio (D-OR), for one, is upset. DeFazio told Egan that "decks at Japanese mills are piled high as Mount Fuji with logs from the Northwest, while mills here at home are scraping for leftovers. . . . We're facing the greatest timber supply crisis in our history while Japanese mills are running around the clock."

Spurred by such tough competition, U.S. companies have pressured the government to allow them to cut more timber from national forests—the only lands from which the export of raw logs has so far been banned. To conservationists' dismay, the Forest Service has obliged industry. "For generations, the Forest Service was seen as the protector of the national forests, and the agency insists it still is," writes Egan. "But some conservationists think the agency has become too cozy in recent years with the timber industry. 'Smokey the Bear has become Mr. Lumberjack,' is how one conservationist group put it."

Many professional planners and managers who work for the U.S. Forest Service agree. After years of silent but uncomfortable complicity, they are now publicly complaining that we are overcutting our national forests. In 1989, former Forest Service timber-sales planner Jeff De Boris told the Chief of the Agency that "we are incurring negative, cumulative impacts to our watersheds, fisheries, and wildlife in our quest to meet our timber targets." By the end of the year, other senior foresters had voiced similar worries. Among the pessimists, the fear is that the kinder, gentler forestry now being advocated for the Pacific old-growth forests is a nice idea whose time has both come and gone. "It's too late," De Boris told *Sierra* magazine in 1990. "It would have worked if they had done it 50 years ago, but now we need all uncut Forest Service land for gene pools and wildlife corridors. I'm not sure we can continue cutting and ensure biological diversity.''

Tensions between those who want to cut old-growth forests and those who want to save them became national news in the United States a few years ago when conservationists looking for a legal way to halt the fast-paced harvest mounted a campaign to save the northern spotted owl, a bird that thrives in these forests but nowhere else and that, much like the proverbial canary in the mine shaft, functions as an indicator of the forest ecosystem's health. A bit like the bald eagle, the spotted owl now stands for the American wilderness and for all the other species that would die out if it went. But even more than biological diversity is at stake in a controversy that has come to focus on a single species. Old-growth forests are also the basis of tourism and recreation opportunities that currently earn the Pacific Northwest more than $6 billion a year. And, because these forests are important watersheds, the region's water quantity and quality, and some of its fisheries, are at risk.

Responding to pressure and lawsuits from environmentalists, the U.S. Fish and Wildlife Service listed the spotted owl as a threatened species in June of 1990. The designation may mean the Forest Service will have to prohibit logging on all its old-growth forests. Meanwhile, the Forest Service has set aside 374,000 acres of national forest for the owl—enough, it claims, to support the 1,300 pairs of birds that nest there. Conservationists believe this is too little; the timber industry thinks it's too big.

Also in 1990, Congress lifted two court injunctions that had been imposed to save the spotted owl by limiting further cutting in Oregon and Washington. About 60 percent of the lands restricted under the court orders were released for cutting, while 40 percent came under protection. The compromise is viewed as only a temporary measure by conservationists, who consider the 60/40 split a losing proposition for the forest.

Industry claims that making life safe for the spotted owl will cost thousands of jobs. Conservationists argue that these jobs are doomed anyway—if logging of old-growth forests continues, there will soon be no large trees left to cut—and that it makes more

sense to manage these types of forests for their value as wildlife habitats and providers of other ecosystem services. An added factor is that many loggers are losing their jobs to automation: it takes roughly four workers to harvest and process the same amount of wood that required five workers just a decade or so ago. In Oregon alone, the industry itself eliminated more than 15,000 jobs in plywood and sawmills between 1979 and 1985.

Although it is an ecologically and symbolically important

species, the spotted owl may in one sense be a red herring. As John Judas writes in *In These Times,* the bottom line is that two strategies of economic growth in the timber industry are competing against each other in the Northwest. The large timber companies are trying to maximize financial returns by exporting raw logs. Meanwhile, people like Representative Peter DeFazio (D-OR) and such groups as International Wood Workers are trying to save jobs by banning the export of unprocessed logs, allowing only finished wood products to be exported.

Unfortunately, there's not a lot of room for compromise, and a choice between maximizing short-term profits and maintaining long-term employment and community stability in forest towns and an ecological balance in the forests themselves now stares us in the face.

According to Jeff Olson, a Wilderness Society economist, the United States loses between four and five jobs for every 1 million board feet of wood exported as raw logs. Following this formula, the 3.7 billion board feet exported as unprocessed logs in 1988 cost 15,000 to 18,000 American jobs. The Oregon Natural Resources Council estimates that, if the United States were to ban all export of raw logs *and* limit logging in the ancient forests of the North-west, the number of jobs saved would almost exactly offset the number lost. At a distance, it's pretty clear which strategy poses the greater risk to jobs, forests, and species. But a way of life is at stake, too, so the spotted owl's fate remains an emotionally charged issue.

As Congress moved toward adjournment in October 1990, the Senate voted on three pieces of legislation aimed at preserving national forests. After prolonged debate, Senators defeated by a vote of 62 to 34 an amendment that would have let the Forest Service exempt the spotted owl from safeguards written into the Endangered Species Act. The other initiatives did not fare so well. Despite opposition mounted by an alliance of environmental groups and fiscal conservatives, the Senate upheld an 1888 law that allows miners who stake claims on federal land to buy up the land for a song—as little as $2.50 an acre. It also tabled a proposal to cut funds for road-building in national forests by nearly $100 million.

Given the long history of federal policy that allows western

Forest violence

miners, timber companies, and ranchers to use public lands while paying the treasury only a fraction of their actual worth, it is more surprising that one attempt to protect national forests succeeded than that two went down to defeat. It remains to be seen whether the hastily assembled alliance that carried the day for the spotted owl and its habitat will prove any match for the longstanding alliance of western Senators the next time decisions about the fate of national forests come to the Senate floor.

Meanwhile, to the north, the Tongass National Forest in Southeast Alaska shelters the last significant stands of temperate rain forest in the Northern Hemisphere. The Tongass encompasses nearly 17 million acres, which makes it three times larger than any other U.S. national forest. It is home to the country's greatest concentrations of bald eagles and grizzly bears, and it helps support the world's biggest salmon fishery, a mainstay of the Alaskan economy. It also shelters the beautiful Inside Passage, a series of waterways, inlets, and islands frequented every year by tourists.

Despite these riches, Tongass has become the biggest drain on

THE FAR SIDE   By GARY LARSON

"And see this ring right here, Jimmy? . . .
That's another time when the old fellow
miraculously survived some big forest fire."

the U.S. Treasury of all national forests, operating deeply in the red, thanks in part to long-term giveaway concessions that the U.S. government has granted to timber concerns. Contributing to these steep losses of money are incentives to build and stabilize employment in southeastern Alaska's timber industry. A strong force has been the *Alaskan National Interest Lands Conservation Act* (ANILCA) of 1980. Passed in the final weeks of a lame-duck administration in a tough bargaining session, during which any thought of wise forest management was overwhelmed by political momentum, the Act set a per-decade production goal of 4.5 billion board feet of timber. ANILCA also provides upwards of $40 million a year ($67 million in 1990) for such pump-priming activities as timber sales preparation and road building.

Environmental groups and many Forest Service employees smell forest death in the ambitious production goal and the grease-the-skids fund. A production goal this high diverts Forest Service energies from recreation and research, they say, and cutting at such a breakneck pace simply can't go on for long. What's more, the fund resembles the type of government logging subsidies that the U.S. government has criticized in other countries. Various bills to improve timber management in the Tongass have come before Congress. But progress is painfully slow, largely because the Alaskan delegation has repeatedly stalled efforts at reform.

As if all of this controversy weren't complicated enough, concern about the release of the tremendous amounts of carbon stored in old-growth forests is also mounting. Scientists from the Forest Service and Oregon State University have shown that, when old-growth trees are harvested, close to 60 percent of the carbon they contain is likely to wind up in the atmosphere almost immediately. The carbon absorbed into the air comes from tops of trees and branches left to rot, exposed soil churned up by logging equipment, smoke from timber processing, or the use of such short-lived products as paper. In one way or another, harvesting 1 acre of old-growth forest adds some 450 tons of carbon dioxide—the main greenhouse gas behind global warming—to the atmosphere over the following 60 years. On a per-acre basis, these forests contain more biomass, and thus more stored carbon, than even Brazil's lush rain forests contain.

The parallels between what's happening in U.S. old-growth forests and in the tropical forests of Asia, Africa, and Latin America are striking. Like many Third World governments, our own is subsidizing the wholesale sell-off of a major natural resource to realize short-term profits. Like many Third World nations, we are selling this resource raw and at cut rates to another country (in this case, Japan), where the "real money" is made processing the wood and, in some cases, selling it back to the supplier country (*us*). Considering that we are already in moral and political quicksand—advising Brazil to leave Amazonian forests intact while felling our own old-growth forests as fast as technology and the Forest Service allow—it's time to take a stand against taking the last stands.

APPENDIX 1

ORGANIZATIONS THAT CAN HELP

Conservation and Environmental Groups

The Children's Rainforest
P.O. Box 936
Lewiston, ME 04240
(207) 784-1069
Educates children on tropical forestry issues and collects money to purchase land in the International Children's Rainforest in Costa Rica.

Conservation International
1015 18th Street, NW
Suite 1000
Washington, DC 20036
(202) 429-5660
Works to preserve biological diversity and ecological systems. Membership is a contribution of $15 or more and includes quarterly newsletter, other publications, and travel opportunities.

Coordinating Body for Indigenous People's
Organizations of the Amazon Basin
1011 Orleans Street
New Orleans, LA 70116
Based in Lima, Peru, this group represents 1.2 million indigenous people in Peru, Bolivia, Ecuador, Colombia, and Brazil.

Cultural Survival
11 Divinity Avenue
Cambridge, MA 02138
(617) 495-2562
Helps to preserve the societies of tribal and ethnic minorities around the world; markets products from tropical forests. Quarterly magazine comes with $25 membership; books, publications, and slide show ($25 rental fee) available.

Earth First!
Tropical Timber Project

c/o Bay Area Earth First!
P.O. Box 83
Canyon, NY 94516
Provides information on tropical forest issues and organization activities. *Earth First Journal* available for $20 from P.O. Box 7, Canton, NY 13617.

Environmental Action Foundation
1525 New Hampshire Avenue, NW
Washington, DC 20036
(202) 745-4870
Promotes environmental protection through research, public education, organizing, and legal action; is connected to Environmental Action, Inc., a national citizens' group. Magazine subscription ($20) includes membership.

Environmental Defense Fund
1616 P Street, NW
Washington, DC 20036
(202) 387-3500
Seeks solutions to ecological problems and enforcement of environmental standards, sometimes through litigation. Focuses on greenhouse effect, ocean pollution, protection of wildlife, recycling, rain forests, acid rain, Antarctica, and toxic waste.

Friends of the Earth
218 D Street, SE
Washington, DC 20003
(202) 544-2600
With affiliate groups in 38 countries, works to influence public policy on environmental issues. Membership ($25) includes news magazine and discounts on publications.

Global Releaf
The American Forestry Association
P.O. Box 2000
Washington, DC 20013
(202) 667-3300
American Forestry Association (AFA) program to encourage tree planting. Information kit comes with guide to tree planting and information on organizing activities to foster awareness of forestry

issues. AFA membership ($24) includes magazine, issue updates, tours, and information on getting involved.

Global Tomorrow Coalition
1325 G Street, NW
Suite 915
Washington, DC 20005
(202) 628-4016
National alliance of organizations and individuals working to preserve equitable life on earth. Offers classroom materials, issue and legislative updates, publications, and slide shows on population, resources, environment, and development issues.

Greenpeace
1436 U Street, NW
Washington, DC 20009
(202) 462-1177
Promotes activism and awareness of environmental issues. Membership ($20) includes bimonthly magazine; network keeps members informed of activities and letter-writing campaigns in their area. Speakers and catalogue of merchandise available.

National Audubon Society
801 Pennsylvania Avenue, SE
Washington, DC 20003
(202) 547-9009
Involved in protecting wildlife and preserving habitats, research, education, and in maintaining over 80 Audubon sanctuaries. Slide shows, technical reports, classroom materials, speakers available.

National Wildlife Federation
1400 16th Street, NW
Washington, DC 20036
(202) 797-6800
Promotes wise use of natural resources. Membership ($20) includes subscription to two magazines, books at discount, educational opportunities, and summer programs. Magazines for children also available: *Big Backyard* for preschoolers ($10) and *Ranger Rick* ($14) for older children.

Natural Resources Defense Council
1350 New York Avenue, NW

Washington, DC 20005
(202) 783-7800
Conducts research, takes legal action on environmental issues (including preservation of Hawaiian forests), and provides legislative updates. Membership ($10) brings quarterly journal and newsletter.

The Nature Conservancy
1815 North Lynn Street
Arlington, VA 22209
(703) 841-5300
Seeks to preserve rare and endangered species through protection of ecosystems; manages more than 1,000 natural preserves. Membership ($15) includes magazine.

Rainforest Action Network
300 Broadway
Suite 28
San Francisco, CA 94133
(415) 398-4404
Urges the protection of U.S. tropical forests and a halt to the funding of projects by the World Bank that harm tropical forests. Subscription ($25 regular; $15 student, low income) includes monthly newsletter.

Rainforest Alliance
295 Madison Avenue
Suite 1804
New York, NY 10017
Provides educational materials, newsletter, and opportunities to travel to tropical forests.

Sierra Club
730 Polk Street
San Francisco, CA 94009
(415) 776-2211
Promotes conservation through public policy. Membership ($33 regular; $15 student, senior, low income) includes magazine and discounts on books and calendars. Publications, outings, calendars, newsletters, national news updates available.

Smithsonian Institution
National Museum of Natural History

Washington, DC 20560
(202) 357-1300
Provides speakers and technical reports on environmental issues.

Smithsonian Institution
National Zoological Park
Washington, DC 20560
(202) 673-4800
Provides classroom materials, speakers, and technical reports.

Southeast Alaska Conservation Council
P.O. Box 021692
Juneau, AK 99802
(907) 586-6942
Regional conservation coalition dedicated to protecting the southeast Alaskan environment.

Survival International
2121 Decatur Place, NW
Washington, DC 20008
(202) 265-1077
Dedicated to preserving the cultures and environments of indigenous peoples. Membership ($20 regular; $10 student, senior) includes newsletter. Based in England, checks should be sent to 310 Edgware Road, London W2 1DY.

The Wilderness Society
1400 Eye Street, NW
Washington, DC 20005
(202) 842-3400
Promotes conservation of such U.S. preserves as the Tongass National Forest, wildlife refuges, the Western wilderness areas, forests of the Pacific Northwest, and national parks. Membership ($15) includes magazine, newsletters, and booklet of Ansel Adams prints.

Wildlife Conservation International
New York Zoological Society
Bronx Zoo
Bronx, NY 10460
(212) 220-5155
Speakers, newsletter, and technical information available.

World Conservation Union (IUCN)
Avenue Mont Blanc
1196 Gland
Switzerland
International federation of government and nongovernmental environment organizations that can provide classroom materials, publications, and technical reports on natural resource issues.

World Resources Institute
1709 New York Avenue, NW
Washington, DC 20006
(202) 638-6300
Independent research center focusing on resource, environment, and development issues. Copublisher of "Tropical Forests: A Call for Action," WRI has worked with international agencies to develop a $5.3 billion, five-year program for the 56 countries most critically affected by tropical deforestation.

Worldwatch Institute
1776 Massachusetts Avenue, NW
Washington, DC 20036
(202) 452-1999
Provides information and publications on a range of issues, including the environment, population, and development.

World Wildlife Fund/
Conservation Foundation
1250 24th Street, NW
Washington, DC 20037
(202) 293-4800
Works to preserve tropical forests and wildlife in Latin America, Africa, and Asia. Membership ($15) brings newsletter, updates on wildlife issues, legislative information, and opportunities to visit project sites and to attend slide shows.

United States Congress

House of Representatives
Committee on Agriculture
1301 Longworth House Office
Washington, DC 20515-6001

Committee on Appropriations
Washington, DC 20515-6015

Committee on Banking, Finance
and Urban Affairs
2129 Rayburn House Office
Building
Washington, DC 20515-6050

Committee on Budget
House Office Building Annex 1
300 New Jersey Avenue, SE
Washington, DC 20515-6065

Committee on Energy and
Commerce
2125 Rayburn House Office
Building
Washington, DC 20515-6115

Committee on Foreign Affairs
2170 Rayburn House Office
Building
Washington, DC 20515-6128

Committee on Government
Operations
2157 Rayburn House Office
Building
Washington, DC 20515-6143

Committee on Interior and
Insular Affairs
1324 Longworth House Office
Building
Washington, DC 20515-6201

Committee on Merchant Marine
and Fisheries
1334 Longworth House Office
Building
Washington, DC 20515-6230

Committee on Public Works
and Transportation
2165 Rayburn House Office
Building
Washington, DC 20515-6256

Committee on Science, Space
and Technology
Washington, DC 20515-6301

Committee on Ways and Means
1102 Longworth House Office
Building
Washington, DC 20515-6348

Senate

Committee on Agriculture,
Nutrition and Forestry
328A Senate Russell Office
Building
Washington, DC 20510-6000

Committee on Appropriations
Washington, DC 20510-6025

Committee on Banking,
Housing and Urban Affairs
534 Senate Dirksen Office
Building
Washington, DC 20510-6075

Committee on Budget
621 Senate Dirksen Office
Building
Washington, DC 20510-6100

Committee on Commerce,
  Science and Transportation
Washington, DC 20510-6125

Committee on Energy and
  Natural Resources
364 Senate Dirksen Office
  Building
Washington, DC 20510-6150

Committee on Environment and
  Public Works
458 Senate Dirksen Office
  Building
Washington, DC 20510-6175

Committee on Finance
205 Senate Dirksen Office
  Building
Washington, DC 20510-6200

United States Agency for International Development

Administrator
United States Agency for International Development
320 21st Street, NW
Washington, DC 20523

Inter-American Development Bank

External Relations Advisor
Inter-American Development Bank
1300 New York Avenue, NW
Washington, DC 20577

World Bank

Director of Environment
World Bank
1818 H Street, NW
Washington, DC 20043

U.S. Executive Director
World Bank
1818 H Street, NW
Washington, DC 20043

U.S. Secretary of Treasury*
1500 Pennsylvania Avenue, NW
Room 3330
Washington, DC 20220

* U.S. policy at the World Bank is often funneled through the U.S.
  Treasury Department.

APPENDIX 2

FORESTS AND GENETIC DIVERSITY

Even if rescued from extinction at the last perilous minute, a species that has been reduced to a fraction of its original population loses much of what once made it unique. In all organisms that reproduce sexually, each individual plant or animal contains a different mix of genes. Known as *genetic diversity,* this incredible variation within species is what allows populations to adapt to changes in climate and other local environmental conditions. When a species—be it bison, goldfish, or daisies—loses too many individuals, it becomes genetically uniform and far less adaptable.

World agriculture will be hard hit if the genes lodged in forests and other wild ecosystems are lost. Time and again, wild tropical species have come to the rescue of their domesticated relatives. Genetic diversity boosts the total crop values on American farms by some $520 million a year, and, without a constant infusion of new hardy genes into our crop species, pests and diseases could quickly get out of hand. Already, more than 400 species of crop pests have developed resistance to one or more of the pesticides used to control them.

Genetic diversity can also be critical in controlling disease. In 1970, for example, the United States lost 15 percent of its corn crop, worth about $1 billion, when a fungus spread rapidly across the Midwest. In this case, genetic uniformity allowed a disease that is always present at low levels, even in the best of years, to run wild. Individual plants were virtually identical and thus genetically defenseless. Only introducing new corn varieties containing new genes stopped the fungus in its tracks. In another instance in the United States, the South's sugarcane industry was saved from near collapse by a gene from a wild Asian species. Genes from a single species of wild rice found in India protects Asian crops from the four major rice diseases. And a barley plant from Ethiopia has provided genes that protect California's $160-million barley crop from the lethal yellow dwarf virus. Wild relatives of crop plants have also helped boost the yields and market appeal of our most important crops.

The true boundlessness of the genetic diversity that plant breeders work with tasks the imagination. "Each species is the repository of an immense amount of genetic information," writes E. O. Wilson in *Biodiversity*. "The number of genes range from about 1,000 in bacteria and 10,000 in some fungi to 700,000 or more in many flowering plants and a few animals. A typical mammal such as the house mouse has about 100,000 genes. . . . If stretched out fully, the DNA would be roughly one meter long. But this molecule is invisible to the naked eye. . . . The full information contained therein, if translated into ordinary-size letters of printed text, would just about fill all 15 editions of the *Encyclopedia Britannica* published since 1768." Tropical biologist Daniel Janzen of the University of Pennsylvania carries this bookish analogy a little bit further: carelessly destroying tropical forests and the species and genes they contain, he says, "is like pulping the Library of Congress to get newsprint."

GLOSSARY

Acid rain (acid precipitation)   The tiny acidic particles of sulfur and nitrogen in air pollution that fall back to earth in rain, snow, clouds, or by themselves. These particles come mainly from the burning of fuels in power plants and motor vehicles. (A more technical term that also includes dry particles is *acid deposition*.)

Afforestation   The planting of trees on once-forested or never-before forested lands.

Biodiversity   All living organisms and the ecological complexes of which they are a part; in other words, the variety of the world's species and genes.

Biota   All of the organisms, including animals, plants, fungi, and microorganisms found in a given area.

Buffer zone   An area next to a protected area where only activities compatible with the objectives of the protected area are allowed; such activities might include tourism, forestry, and some kinds of agriculture. Such zones help protect the reserve and compensate local people who lose access to the reserve's biological resources.

Carrying capacity   The maximum number of organisms that can use a given area of habitat without degrading it and without causing social stresses that cause species to die or to die out. When applied to humans, *carrying capacity* refers to the maximum number of users particular land resources can sustain using particular technology.

Climate change (global warming)   Global warming refers to the changes in the earth's climate resulting from the buildup in the atmosphere of carbon dioxide and other "greenhouse" gases. These gases trap more of the earth's heat and enhance the natural greenhouse effect that keeps the planet from freezing solid and being virtually lifeless. About half of the enhanced warming comes from fossil fuel combustion; the rest comes primarily from deforestation, from the release of chlorofluorocarbons, and from agricultural activities. Expected changes in the climate include an increase in the earth's surface temperature, changes in global precipitation patterns, and a rise in sea levels. These changes could lead to disruptions in agriculture, the flooding of low-lying coastal regions, and the loss of many natural ecosystems. The United States is the largest single emitter of greenhouse gases.

Debt-for-nature swap   Financial arrangements in which part of a nation's external debt is bought at a discount and is then sold back to the government in local currency, with the proceeds used for conservation.

Deforestation   The permanent loss of forestland or its conversion to other land uses (agriculture, cities, etc.).

Ecology   A branch of science concerned with how living organisms are connected to each other and to their environment.

Ecosystem   The organisms of a particular habitat, such as a pond or a forest, together with their physical environment. Ecosystems are ever changing and have no fixed boundaries. Depending upon the purpose, scientists, resource managers, or policymakers consider a single lake, a watershed, or an entire region an ecosystem.

Environment   All the physical, chemical, and biological factors that influence a living organism.

Ex-situ conservation   Conserving germplasm resources (seed, pollen, sperm, individual organisms) by removing them from their original habitat or natural environment and by placing them in seed banks, zoos, and so on.

Extinction   The evolutionary termination of a species caused by the failure to reproduce and the death of all remaining members of the species; the natural failure to adapt to environmental change.

Fauna   The total animal life of an area; usually, the total number of animal species in a specified period, geological stratum, region, ecosystem, habitat, or community at a specific time.

Flora   The total plant life of an area; usually, the total number of plant species in a geological stratum, region, ecosystem, habitat, or community at a specific time.

Gene   The functional unit of heredity; the part of the DNA molecule that encodes a single enzyme or structural protein unit.

Genetic diversity   Variation in the genetic composition of individuals within or among species populations.

Habitat   The environment in which an organism lives.

Indigenous   Originating, reproducing, growing, or living naturally in a particular region or environment; native.

In-situ conservation   Conserving genes or species in their natural setting, that is, where they evolved.

Natural resources   All renewable resources (forests, water, wildlife, soils, etc.) and nonrenewable (oil, coal, iron ore, etc.) resources that occur in nature.

Nongovernmental organizations   All community, citizen, public-interest, or voluntary groups except trade associations and businesses.

Old-growth forests (nicknamed "green cathedrals")   Forests with trees that are from 250 to over 1,000 years old and have downed logs or standing snags. Some trees in such forests reach heights of 300 feet and diameters of 6 feet.

Photosynthesis   The process by which simple carbohydrates (sugars and starches) are formed from carbon dioxide, water, and essential nutrients in special plant cells using sunlight as the energy source.

Protected area   Any area of land protected by laws or regulations that limit human use of the plants and animals within that area; includes national parks, game reserves, and so on.

Reforestation   The replanting of deforested lands.

Snag   Standing dead tree.

Species   A population or a group of populations of organisms that can interbreed freely with each other but not with members of other species.

Species diversity (or species richness)   A function of the distribution and abundance of species; an ecosystem is more diverse if the species present have equal population sizes and less diverse if many species are rare and some are very common.

Sustainable development   A process of social and economic change in which resource use, technology, and custom are all in harmony, enabling the current generation to meet its needs and hopes without compromising those of future generations.

Watershed   An area bounded by waters that part and drain to one or more rivers or other watercourses.

SELECTED READINGS

"Amazonia: Deforestation and Possible Effects," *Interciencia*. (Special issue.) November/December 1989.

American Forestry Association. *American Forests*. (Special issue on tropical deforestation.) November/December 1988.

Anderson, Dennis. *The Economics of Afforestation: A Case Study in Africa*. (Occasional Paper Number 1/New Series.) Washington, DC and Baltimore: World Bank and Johns Hopkins University Press, October 1987.

Annis, Sheldon. "Debt and Wrong-Way Resource Flows in Costa Rica." *Ethics and International Affairs,* vol. 4, 1990, pp. 107–121.

———"Costa Rica's Dual Debt: A Story About a Little Country That Did Things Right." Washington, DC: World Resources Institute, June 1987.

Brown, Lester, et al. *State of the World 1989*. (A Worldwatch Institute publication.) New York and Oxford: W. W. Norton, 1989.

———. *State of the World 1990*. (A Worldwatch Institute publication.) New York and Oxford: W. W. Norton, 1990.

Callahan, North. *TVA: Bridge Over Troubled Waters*. New York: A. S. Barnes, 1980.

Castner, James L. *Rainforests: A Guide to Research and Tourist Facilities at Selected Tropical Forest Sites in Central and South America*. Florida: Feline Press, 1990.

Caufield, Catherine. "The Ancient Forest." *The New Yorker,* May 14, 1990, pp. 46–84.

———. *In the Rainforest*. Chicago: University of Chicago Press, 1986.

Chandler, William. *The Myth of TVA*. Washington, DC: Environmental Policy Institute, 1984.

195

Clary, David A. *Timber and the Forest Service.* Lawrence, KS: University Press of Kansas, 1986.

Colinvaux, Paul A. "The Past and Future Amazon." *Scientific American,* May 1989, pp. 102–108.

Collingwood, G. H., et al. *Knowing Your Trees.* Washington, DC: American Forestry Association, 1974.

Denslow, Julie Sloan, and Christine Padoch, eds. *People of the Tropical Rain Forest.* Berkeley and Los Angeles: University of California Press (in association with Smithsonian Institution Traveling Exhibition Service, Washington, DC), 1988.

Dourojeanni, Marc J. *Amazônia ¿Que Hacer?* Iquitos-Peru: Centro de Estudios Teologicos de la Amazônia, 1990.

Durning, Alan B. *Action at the Grassroots: Fighting Poverty and Environmental Decline.* (Worldwatch Paper 88.) Washington, DC: Worldwatch Institute, 1989.

Durrell, Lee. *State of the Ark.* Garden City, NY: Doubleday, 1986.

Ehrlich, Paul. "Facing the Habitability Crisis." *BioScience,* July/August 1989, pp. 480–482.

Ehrlich, Paul, and Anne Ehrlich. *Extinction: The Causes and Consequences of the Disappearance of Species.* New York: Random House, 1981.

Finer, Herman. *The T.V.A.: Lessons for International Application.* Montreal: International Labour Office, 1944.

Food and Agriculture Organization of the United Nations (FAO), United Nations Development Programme, World Bank, and World Resources Institute. *The Tropical Forestry Action Plan.* Rome: FAO, 1987.

Gennino, Angela, ed. *Amazônia: Voices for the Rainforest.* San Francisco: Rainforest Action Network and Amazônia Film Project, 1990.

Gradwohl, Judith, and Russell Greenberg. *Saving the Tropical Forests.* London: Earthscan Publications Limited, 1988.

Hecht, Susanna, and Alexander Cockburn. *The Fate of the Forest: Developers, Destroyers, and Defenders of the Amazon.* London: Verso, 1989.

Jacobs, Marius. *The Tropical Rain Forest: A First Encounter.* Berlin: Springer-Verlag, 1988.

Janzen, Daniel H. "Tropical Ecological and Biocultural Restoration." *Science,* January 15, 1988, pp. 243–244.

Jolly, Alison. *A World Like Our Own: Man and Nature in Madagascar.* New Haven, CT: Yale University Press, 1980.

Kelly, David, and Gary Braasch. *Secrets of the Old Growth Forest.* Salt Lake City: Gibbs Smith, 1988.

King, Laura B., et al. *Extinction in Paradise: Protecting Our Hawaiian Species.* (A report.) New York: Natural Resources Defense Council, 1989.

Leopold, Aldo. *A Sand County Almanac.* New York: Oxford University Press, 1949.

Linden, Eugene. "Torching the Amazon: Can the Rain Forest Be Saved?" *Time,* September 18, 1989: pp. 76–85.

MacKenzie, James J., and Mohamed T. El-Ashry. *Ill Winds: Airborne Pollution's Toll on Trees and Crops.* Washington, DC: World Resources Institute, 1988.

McNeeley, Jeffrey A. *Economics and Biological Diversity: Developing and Using Economic Incentives to Conserve Biological Resources.* Gland, Switzerland: International Union for Conservation of Nature and Natural Resources, 1988.

McNeely, Jeffrey A., et al. *Conserving the World's Biological Diversity.* Gland, Switzerland, and Washington, DC: International Union for Conservation of Nature and Natural Resources, World Resources Institute, World Wildlife Fund-U.S., Conservation International, and World Bank, 1989.

Maguire, Andrew, and Janet Welsh Brown. *Bordering on Trouble: Resources and Politics in Latin America.* (A World Resources Institute book.) Bethesda, MD: Adler & Adler, 1986.

Mahar, Dennis J. *Government Policies and Deforestation in Brazil's Amazon Region.* Washington, DC: World Bank (in cooperation with World Wildlife Fund), January 1989.

Maser, Chris. *Forest Primeval: The Natural History of an Ancient Forest.* San Francisco: Sierra Club, 1989.

Mello, Robert A. *Last Stand of the Red Spruce.* Washington, DC: Island Press (for the National Resources Defense Council), 1987.

Minton, John Dean. *The New Deal in Tennessee.* New York: Garland Publishing, 1979.

Morrison, Peter H. *Old Growth in the Pacific Northwest: A Status Report.* Alexandria, VA: Global Printing, Inc. (for the Wilderness Society), 1987.

Myers, Norman. *Conversion of Tropical Moist Forests.* Washington, DC: National Academy of Sciences, 1980.

————. *The Primary Source: Tropical Forests and Our Future.* New York: W. W. Norton, 1984.

————. *The Sinking Ark.* Oxford: Pergamon Press, 1979.

National Academy of Sciences. *Research Priorities in Tropical Biology.* Washington, DC: National Academy of Sciences, 1980.

National Geographic Society. *Earth 88: Changing Geographic Perspectives.* Washington, DC: National Geographic Society, 1988.

Parfit, Michael. "Whose Heads Will Shape the Future of the Amazon's Green Mansions?" *Smithsonian,* vol 20, no. 8, November 1989, pp. 58–74.

Perry, Donald. *Life Above the Jungle Floor.* New York: Simon & Schuster, 1986.

Pollock, Cynthia. *Mining Urban Wastes: The Potential for Recycling.* (Worldwatch Paper 76.) Washington, DC: Worldwatch Institute, April 1987.

Postel, Sandra, and Lori Heise. *Reforesting the Earth.* (Worldwatch Paper 83.) Washington, DC: Worldwatch Institute, April 1988.

Prescott-Allen, Christine, and Robert Prescott-Allen. *The First Resource.* New Haven, CT: Yale University Press, 1986.

Reid, Walter V., and Kenton R. Miller. *Keeping Options Alive: The Scientific Basis for Conserving Biodiversity.* Washington, DC: World Resources Institute, 1989.

Reid, Walter V., et al. *Bankrolling Successes: A Portfolio of Sustainable Development Projects.* Washington, DC: Environmental Policy Institute and National Wildlife Federation, 1988.

Repetto, Robert. *The Forest for the Trees? Government Policies and the Misuse of Forest Resources.* Washington, DC: World Resources Institute, 1988.

Repetto, Robert, ed. *The Global Possible: Resources, Development and the New Century*. (A World Resources Institute book.) New Haven, CT and London: Yale University Press, 1985.

Repetto, Robert, and Malcolm Gillis, eds. *Public Policies and the Misuse of Forest Resources*. (A World Resources Institute book.) Cambridge: Cambridge University Press, 1988.

Repetto, Robert, et al. *Wasting Assets: Natural Resources in the National Income Accounts*. Washington, DC: World Resources Institute, 1989.

Richards, John F., and Richard P. Tucker, eds. *World Deforestation in the Twentieth Century*. Durham, NC: Duke University Press, 1988.

"Save the Forests: Save the Planet," *The Ecologist* (Special issue), vol. 17, No. 4/5, July/November 1987, pp. 129–208.

Swartzman, Stephen. "Extractive Reserves: Distribution of Wealth and the Social Costs of Frontier Development in the Amazon." (Paper presented to symposium sponsored by National Wildlife Federation, World Wildlife Fund, and Conservation Foundation on "Extractive Economies in Tropical Forests: A Course of Action," November 30 and December 1, 1989, Washington, DC.) Washington, DC: Environmental Defense Fund, 1989.

Shea, Keith R., and Les W. Carlson. *Increasing Productivity of Multipurpose Tree Species: A Blueprint for Action*. Washington, DC: United States Department of Agriculture, Forest Service, July 1984.

Shoumatoff, Alex. *The Rivers Amazon*. San Francisco: Sierra Club, 1986.

Soulé, Michael E. "What Is Conservation Biology?" *BioScience*. December 1985, pp. 727–734.

Soulé, Michael E., ed. *Conservation Biology: The Science of Scarcity and Diversity*. Sunderlane, MA: Sinauer, 1986.

Soulé, Michael E., and Bruce A. Wilcox, eds. *Conservation Biology: An Evolutionary-Ecological Perspective*. Sunderlane, MA: Sinauer, 1980.

Starke, Linda. *Signs of Hope: Working Towards Our Common Future*. (A publication of the Centre for Our Common Future.) New York and London: Oxford University Press, 1990.

Stone, Roger. *Dreams of Amazonia*. New York: Penguin, 1986.

Thurman, Sybil, ed. *History of the Tennessee Valley Authority*. Knoxville, TN: S. B. Newman Printing Co. (for Tennessee Valley Authority Information Office), 1982.

Trexler, Mark, et al. "Forestry as a Response to Global Warming: An Analysis of the Guatemala Agroforestry and Carbon Sequestration Project." Washington, DC: World Resources Institute, 1989.

U.S. Congress, Office of Technology Assessment. *Technologies to Maintain Biological Diversity*. Washington, DC: U.S. Government Printing Office, 1987.

————. *Technologies to Sustain Tropical Forest Resources*. Washington, DC: U.S. Government Printing Office, 1984.

Wilcove, David S. *National Forests: Policies for the Future*. (Wilderness Society report.) Alexandria, VA: Global Printing, Inc., 1988.

Wilderness Society. *End of the Ancient Forests: Special Report on National Forest Plans in the Pacific Northwest*. Alexandria, VA: Global Printing, Inc., 1988.

————. *National Forests: Policies for the Future*. (5 volumes.) Washington, DC: Wilderness Society, 1988.

Wilson, Edward O. *Biophilia*. Cambridge, MA: Harvard University Press, 1984.

Wilson, Edward O., ed. *Biodiversity*. Washington, DC: National Academy Press, 1988.

World Bank. *Madagascar Environmental Action Plan*. Washington, DC: World Bank, July 1988.

World Resources Institute and International Institute for Environment and Development (in collaboration with the United Nations Environment Programme). *World Resources 1988–89*. New York: Basic Books, 1988.

World Resources Institute (in collaboration with the United Nations Environment Programme and the United Nations Development Programme). *World Resources 1990–91*. New York and Oxford: Oxford University Press, 1990.

World Resources Institute, World Bank, and United Nations Development Programme. *Tropical Forests: A Call for Action*. Washington, DC: World Resources Institute, 1989.

World Wildlife Fund (WWF). *WWF List of Approved Projects*. Washington, DC: WWF, 1988.

ABOUT THE AUTHORS

Kenton R. Miller is director of World Resources Institute's Program in Forests and Biodiversity. Prior to joining WRI, Kenton served for five years as director general of the International Union for the Conservation of Nature and Natural Resources. Previously, he directed the Center for Strategic Wildland Management Studies at the University of Michigan and, before that, the United Nations Food and Agriculture Organization's wild lands management activities in Latin America and the Caribbean.

Laura Tangley is a science journalist with a long-standing interest in the conservation of forests and other ecosystems, particularly in the tropics. She has written many articles on these subjects, mostly for *BioScience* magazine, where she was features editor until 1988. Laura is currently associate editor of *Earthwatch* magazine.

INDEX

Acid rain, 9–10, 45
Acre (state, Brazil), 58, 75
  land prices in, 61
Africa, 92–96
Agency for International Development, U.S., 138, 157
  mailing address, 188
Agro-ecological zoning, Northwest Development Pole, 62–63
AID. See Agency for International Development
AIDESEP. See Inter-Ethnic Association for Development Peruvian Tropical Forest
Air pollution, 45–48
  and conservation management, 124–26
Alaska, temperate rain forest in, 177
Alaskan National Interest Lands Conservation Act, 178
Alpine ibex, 150
Altamira Hydroelectric Complex (Brazil), 81
Aluminum, recycling in selected countries, 167
Amatenango del Valle (Mexico), 45
Amazon Basin, 18, 25
  acid rain and consequent damage, 48
Amazon River, 53–54
Amazônia, 53–86
  holistic exhibit of, 152–53
  loss of species in, 21
Amazônia, Que Hacer? (Dourojeanni), 76
Ambio (journal), 71
Ambuklao Dam (Philippines), 14
American bison, reintroduction from zoo stock, 149

American Forestry Association (AFA), 6, 157–58, 168
American Forests, 139–40
American Museum of Natural History, The, 94
Amerindians, 72
  as foreigners in Brazil, 81
Amistad Biosphere Reserve, La, 112
Amnesty International, 76
Animal species, 5
  number according to major group, 20
Annis, Sheldon, 34–35, 114–16
Appalachian Mountains
  forest losses to air pollution, 46
Applied Energy Services, 157
Arabian oryx, reintroduction from zoo stock, 149
Araucaria forests, 61
Argentina, areas on the World Heritage danger list, 129
Arias, Oscar (President, Costa Rica), 113
Arnold Arboretum, 150
Ashton, Peter, 18, 31, 150
Associacíon de las Nuevas Alquimistas Internacional (ANAI), 140–41
Audubon Society, 136, 138–39
Austria, recycling in, 167
Automation, and employment in logging, 175

Babaquara Dam (Brazil), 81
Balbina Dam (Brazil), 63
Bald eagle, 174
Bali, 37
Barco, Virgilio (President, Colombia), 83
Bateson, Gregory, 27

203

ABOUT WRI

World Resources Institute (WRI) is an independent research and policy center in Washington, D.C., that helps governments, other nonprofit organizations, businesses, and citizens look for ways to meet basic human needs and nurture economic growth without degrading our planet and its resources.

The institute's staff of scientists, economists, political scientists, communicators, and others collaborate in five broad programs: climate, energy, and pollution; economics and institutions; resource and environmental information; forests, biodiversity, and sustainable agriculture; and technology and the environment. It also provides developing countries with technical assistance in resource assessment, planning, and management.

WRI is funded by private foundations, the United Nations, international government agencies, corporations, and concerned individuals.

World Resources Institute
1709 New York Ave., NW
Washington, DC 20006

7465

DATE DUE